Kirk Scott

University of Alaska Anchorage

 **the**

SQL
Programming Language

JONES AND BARTLETT PUBLISHERS

Sudbury, Massachusetts

BOSTON   TORONTO   LONDON   SINGAPORE

World Headquarters

Jones and Bartlett Publishers
40 Tall Pine Drive
Sudbury, MA 01776
978-443-5000
info@jbpub.com
www.jbpub.com

Jones and Bartlett Publishers
Canada
6339 Ormindale Way
Mississauga, Ontario L5V 1J2
Canada

Jones and Bartlett Publishers
International
Barb House, Barb Mews
London W6 7PA
United Kingdom

Jones and Bartlett's books and products are available through most bookstores and online booksellers. To contact Jones and Bartlett Publishers directly, call 800-832-0034, fax 978-443-8000, or visit our website www.jbpub.com.

Substantial discounts on bulk quantities of Jones and Bartlett's publications are available to corporations, professional associations, and other qualified organizations. For details and specific discount information, contact the special sales department at Jones and Bartlett via the above contact information or send an email to special-sales@jbpub.com.

Production Credits
Publisher: David Pallai
Acquisitions Editor: Timothy Anderson
Editorial Assistant: Melissa Potter
Production Director: Amy Rose
Production Assistant: Ashlee Hazeltine
Senior Marketing Manager: Andrea DeFronzo
V.P., Manufacturing and Inventory Control: Therese Connell
Composition: Northeast Compositors
Title Page and Cover Design: Scott Moden
Title Page and Cover Image: © Pitris/Dreamstime.com
Printing and Binding: Malloy, Inc.
Cover Printing: Malloy, Inc.

Library of Congress Cataloging-in-Publication Data
Scott, Kirk.
 The SQL programming language / Kirk Scott. -- 1st ed.
   p. cm.
 Includes bibliographical references.
 ISBN-13: 978-0-7637-6674-0 (pbk.)
 ISBN-10: 0-7637-6674-7 (ibid.)
 1. SQL (Computer program language) I. Title.
 QA76.73.S67S38 2009
 005.13'3--dc22

                         2009010209

6048
Printed in the United States of America
13 12 11 10 09   10 9 8 7 6 5 4 3 2 1

contents

About This Book

The *SQL Programming Language* discusses SQL, or Structured Query Language. This language can be used to define and manage the data in a relational database. This means that SQL can be used to create tables, enter data into them, and retrieve that data later on. This book consists of six chapters of text, an accompanying example database, and exercises.

In a work this short, it isn't possible to cover all of the topics related to SQL. Instead, the book is selective and focuses on those points that would be of most value to someone who is being introduced to SQL for the first time. Many books start by creating tables and entering data into them. This book takes the point of view that, for a beginner, it is more useful to first learn how to use a database that has already been created by someone else.

Chapters 1 and 2 discuss basic ideas underlying the design of a relational database. The goal of these chapters is to give all of the information necessary to understand the example database, so that it is possible to write queries to retrieve information from it.

Chapters 3 through 5 introduce the most important and useful features of SQL as a query language, building from simple to more complex subjects. Each chapter is broken into short subsections, each of which covers one concept and the related SQL keywords and syntax. The philosophy of the book is that SQL is best learned by example. Most of the subsections contain one or more example queries.

At the ends of Chapters 3 through 5, problem queries are stated in English. The reader's task is to translate these queries into SQL, using the examples given in the chapter as models. Answers can be checked by trying to run them against the example database. All of the examples and solutions to the problems are included in the example database.

Chapter 6 briefly explains how tables can be created and data entered into them using SQL. For the interested reader, a complete set of SQL statements for creating and populating the example database is available for downloading.

About the Example Database

The example database is given as a Microsoft Access database. It can be downloaded from http://www.jbpub.com/catalog/9780763766740. To use the database, you must have a version of Microsoft Access installed. Essentially, the only feature of Microsoft Access needed to make full use of this book is its SQL editor. It is not difficult to access and use the editor, but different versions of Access have different graphical user interfaces. It's not practical to show how to find the SQL editor for every version. However, every version of Access has a Help option in the main menu; searching the Help menu with the term "SQL view" will give the needed information.

SQL is an international standard. Microsoft Access adheres to the standard while adding some useful features. Among the features in Access are the data types known as TEXT, NUMBER, and CURRENCY. These data types are simple and useful, especially for the beginner. In Access it is possible to set off date values using the # symbol rather than the ' symbol—another useful convention for the beginner. These features are used in the example database. In theory, it would be possible to use this book with a different database management system, but you would need to convert the example database to the other system. This could prove difficult because of differences in data types and other differences between Access and that system. It would also be necessary to make some minor changes in the example queries and the problem solutions.

Microsoft Access maintains uppercase (capital) and lowercase (small) letters in the stored data, but the SQL language itself is not case sensitive. Certain simple conventions are used in the example queries and problem solutions of this book that should make the SQL queries easier to read and understand. The example database consists of tables containing information about movies, actors, the roles they played, and so on. In the example queries, SQL keywords are given in all uppercase letters. The names of tables and columns are not capitalized, except for certain letters. The first letter of the names of tables is capitalized. For example, the table containing data about movies is known as the Movie table. If a table has a compound name, then the first letter of each part of the name is capitalized—for example, RoleQuote. Tables contain columns. The Movie table, for example, has columns named title, movieID, awardsWon, and DVDPrice. These names illustrate the following conventions: The first letter of a column name is not capitalized unless it's part of an acronym; acronyms are uppercase. If the column name is a compound name, the first letters of any parts after the first part are capitalized.

Relational Databases, Entities, Tables, and Primary Keys

1.1 Relational Databases and Entities

A relational database is a means of storing data so that it can be retrieved as useful information. The design of a database rests on the concept of an entity, something that you would like to store information about. For example, if you were interested in storing information about the motion picture industry, you might like to store information about actors, movies, and the roles actors played in specific movies. Actors and movies are examples of concrete entities. Roles, and the relationship between actors and movies that they embody, are more abstract in nature. They are still entities, however, so it is also possible to store information about roles in a database.

1.2 Entities, Attributes, Tables, Rows, and Columns

For any kind of entity, such as a movie, there are individual instances of it. Each movie can be described by a set of characteristics, or attributes. For example, a movie has a title, it is released in a given year, it is produced by a given production company, and so on. Similarly, an actor has a name, a date of birth, and so on. A relational database uses tables to store information about entities and their attributes. Each row in the table contains information about one instance of an entity, and each column contains the value for a specific attribute of an entity.

Table 1.1 is a small example of a Movie table. Each row in the table represents one movie. The table has columns named title, year, and company, which contain information about the movie. It also has a special column, movieID, which contains an arbitrary, unique identifier for each movie.

TABLE 1.1 Movie

movieID	title	year	company
001	Apollo 13	1995	Imagine Entertainment and Universal Pictures
002	Casablanca	1943	Warner Brothers
003	Dirty Harry	1971	The Malpaso Company

1.3 Primary Keys and Entity Integrity

A table should not contain duplicate rows. This idea has important implications. Consider Table 1.2, a simple example of a Role table.

TABLE 1.2 Role

roleName
Batman
Batman

Repeating Batman in the Role table is both a waste of space and a potential source of confusion. It is not clear what the repetition of Batman might mean. Put simply, having two rows in a table that are exactly the same adds no information to the database.

Now consider Table 1.3, the expanded Role table. It contains an additional column, roleID. Batman again appears twice, but the rows in which this role-Name appears are different because the roleID values in the rows are different. This repetition is not a waste of space; it adds information. The Batman role appears in different movies. Because the movies are different and the actor who plays them may be different, these two roles—even though they have the same name—are considered different. Giving them unique roleID values makes it possible to distinguish between the two different roles with the same name. The repetition of the name tells you that a role with the same name appeared in two different movies.

TABLE 1.3 Role

roleID	roleName
00095	Batman
00097	The Joker
00106	Batman

The roleID column in the Role table plays a critical part in the design and use of the table. A column that contains a unique identifier for each row in a table is known as the primary key. Every table has to have a primary key. In most cases, the primary key is a single column in the table. Less frequently, the primary key consists of a combination of columns in the table. For every row, the primary key column has to contain a value, and this value is required to be unique. This requirement is so important that it is given a name: entity integrity. If entity integrity is maintained, then every row in a table is different, and it becomes possible to retrieve the information from a specific row without confusion.

1.4 Table Schema Notation

A schema is a plan or design for a table in a database. Schema notation serves as a convenient summary of a table, giving its name and the names of its columns. It shows the structure of a table without showing its contents. Schema notation can also indicate the primary key of a table. Suppose "pk" is an abbreviation that follows the name of the column that serves as the primary key of a table. Then the schema notation for the Role table as given in Table 1.3 looks like this:

```
Role(roleID pk, roleName)
```

This notation will be expanded shortly to include other useful information about the table.

1.5 The Text and Number Data Types

Data types refer to the kinds of values that can be stored in the columns of a table. The two most basic data types are text and numbers. The title of a movie is an example of text: It consists of combinations of letters, digits, and other printable characters. When defining a text column, it is necessary to specify the maximum number of characters it can contain.

The year a movie was released is an example of a number. If you might conceivably need to add, subtract, multiply, or divide a value, then that value should be stored as a number, not as text. You might want to find how many years passed between the release of a movie and its sequel, for example. This information could be obtained by subtracting the release year of the original from the release year of the sequel. When defining a number column, it is not necessary to specify how many digits it can contain. The system will handle values up to some prespecified maximum.

1.6 The Currency Data Type

Table 1.4 is the Movie table expanded to include a column for the price of a DVD of the movie. The DVDPrice column in the Movie table is of the currency data type. This column contains numeric values, which could be used in arithmetic expressions. The currency data type causes these values to be shown with $ signs and two decimal places.

TABLE 1.4 Movie

movieID	title	year	company	DVDPrice
001	Apollo 13	1995	Imagine Entertainment and Universal Pictures	$12.99
002	Casablanca	1943	Warner Brothers	$19.99
003	Dirty Harry	1971	The Malpaso Company	$16.99

1.7 The Date Data Type

Table 1.5 is an example of an Actor table. The birthDate column in the Actor table contains the date of birth of the actor; it is of the date data type. This column contains American-style dates, with the digits representing the month, day, and year separated by slashes. The date data type is a composite type because it consists of these three parts. It also has a numeric aspect. If you wanted to find out how much older one person is than another person, for example, this goal could be accomplished by finding the differences between the year parts of their birth dates.

TABLE 1.5 Actor

actorID	lastName	firstName	birthDate
00001	Hanks	Tom	7/9/1956
00002	Paxton	Bill	5/17/1955
00003	Bacon	Kevin	7/8/1958

1.8 When Is a Number Not a Number?

The Actor, Movie, and Role tables have primary key columns actorID, movieID, and roleID, respectively. These columns contain values consisting of digits. It is quite common to use digits to form unique identifiers. There are practical reasons for this choice: It is easy to tell how many potential values there are if you know how many digits the column can contain. It is also easy to generate sequences of primary key values one after the other.

Keep in mind that even though the values in these columns consist of digits, the values are not arithmetic numbers. Numbers do not display leading zeros, and there would never be any practical reason to add, subtract, multiply, or divide an identifier value such as actorID, movieID, or roleID. In the designs of these tables, the primary key columns are defined to have the text data type, not the number data type. This approach is good practice because it prevents users from mistakenly trying to do arithmetic on a value that is not actually a number.

1.9 More Complete Schema Notation

Detailed schemas of table designs include the data types for each of the columns in the tables. The maximum number of characters in a text column is put in parentheses after the word "text." The indication of the primary key column is retained. This is spelled out rather than using the abbreviation "pk." Here are schemas for the tables as given so far:

Movie

(movieID	text(3)	primary key,
title	text(36),	
year	number,	
company	text(50),	
DVDPrice	currency)	

Actor

(actorID	text(5)	primary key,
lastName	text(24),	
firstName	text(24),	
birthDate	date)	

Role

(roleID	text(4)	primary key,
roleName	text(36))	

1.10 The Definition of Null

Table 1.6 is an expanded version of the Actor table. It includes a column for date of death. At the time of writing, the three actors given in the table were alive, so no value is stored in the deathDate column. The term "null" is used to describe this situation. A nonvalue is known as null. For example, you would say that the value of the deathDate column for Tom Hanks is null, and likewise for the other actors in the table.

TABLE 1.6 Actor

actorID	lastName	firstName	birthDate	deathDate
00001	Hanks	Tom	7/9/1956	
00002	Paxton	Bill	5/17/1955	
00003	Bacon	Kevin	7/8/1958	

Although it makes perfect sense for the deathDate column to contain null values, not all columns are allowed to be null. The requirement that a table have a primary key column and that every row have a value in that column can be stated in terms of null values. Entity integrity requires that the primary key column of a table can never be null. If null values were allowed, then the column could not serve as a unique identifier.

1.11 Data Integrity

In addition to being part of the phrase "entity integrity," the term "integrity" is used in a more general way when talking about databases. The phrase "data integrity" refers to the requirement that the data stored in a table must be correct. Most databases do not attain this goal completely. Incorrect data can arise from simple mistakes, such as typographical errors. Incorrect data can also arise when information sources conflict and the creator of a database has to make a choice about which value to accept and use. When creating the database for this book, the sources that were used conflicted with each other in some cases. When different sources gave different birth dates, for example, it was necessary to choose one, knowing that there was some doubt about the correct value.

It is also desirable for the contents of a database to be as complete as possible. Of course, sources of information may be incomplete, and it makes no sense to knowingly include values that are simply guesses. In some cases, the sources of information for the examples in this book gave only a year of birth for an actor, not a date of birth. Because the birthDate column is defined to contain a date, not just a year, in those cases the column was left blank. This is a valid use of null values, but ideally it should happen only infrequently.

The bottom line is that perfection can rarely be achieved. A reasonably complete and correct database can be a great convenience in making data available as useful information. Even so, it is better to have no database at all than to have a database that is full of false information. False information misleads users into thinking they are retrieving facts when they are only retrieving nonsense. It is up to the person who is responsible for the database, and who enters data into it, to ensure the integrity of the data that it contains.

chapter 2

Entities and Relationships

2.1 Foreign Keys and Relationships between Tables

When a database is designed correctly, information about different kinds of entities is stored in separate tables. The relationships between the entities in different tables are as important as the attributes of the entities themselves. The Actor and Role tables, as introduced in Chapter 1, contained no information telling which actor played which role. In contrast, Table 2.1 shows the Role table expanded to include an actorID column, which captures the relationship between the Actor and Role tables.

TABLE 2.1 Role

roleID	roleName	gender	actorID
00052	Colonel Nathan R. Jessep	M	00019
00095	Batman	M	00076
00097	The Joker	M	00019

Given a Role table containing an actorID column, to find out the actor who played a certain role, you can look up the actorID for the role in Table 2.2, the Actor table. The actorID column in the Actor table is the primary key; the actorID column in the Role table is known as a foreign key. Two tables related in this way are in a primary key to foreign key relationship. Embedding the primary key of one table as a foreign key in another table captures the relationship between the rows of the different tables.

TABLE 2.2 Actor

actorID	lastName	firstName
00019	Nicholson	Jack
00076	Keaton	Michael

2.2 The One-to-Many Relationship and Entity Relationship Diagrams

Primary key to foreign key relationships between entities in two different tables fall into three categories: one-to-many, one-to-one, and many-to-many. The Actor–Role example illustrates a one-to-many relationship. Observe that one actor, Jack Nicholson, plays more than one role, the Joker and Colonel Nathan R. Jessep. In this example, the Actor table can be referred to as the *one* table, and the Role table can be referred to as the *many* table.

The rule of thumb for capturing one-to-many relationships between two tables can be stated in this way: Embed the primary key of the *one* table as a foreign key in the *many* table. It is critically important to embed the primary key of the *one* table as a foreign key in the *many* table, and not the other way around. If the primary key of the Role table were embedded as a foreign key in the Actor table, it would become impossible to record the fact that a given actor had played more than one role.

A convenient notation has been developed for displaying entities and their relationships graphically. Entity relationship diagrams, known as E-R diagrams, represent tables with named rectangles; the relationships between the tables are indicated with lines between those rectangles. If the end of a line does not branch, that represents *one*. If the end of a line branches (known as a crow's foot), that represents *many*. Figure 2.1 is an E-R diagram that graphically illustrates the relationship between the Actor and Role tables: One actor can play many roles.

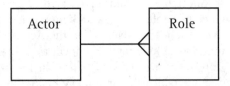

Figure 2.1 *Actor–Role Entity Relationship Diagram*

2.3 The One-to-One Relationship

The one-to-one relationship is a special case of the one-to-many relationship. The Actor–Role example also illustrates this idea. Observe that one actor, Michael Keaton, plays only one role, Batman. This relationship is captured by embedding the primary key of the Actor table as a foreign key in the Role table. If another role were to be recorded for Michael Keaton in the future, there would be no problem. The data in the tables would simply reflect a one-to-many relationship, like Jack Nicholson's, rather than a one-to-one relationship.

If you had a pair of tables in which the entities were always and only in one-to-one relationships with each other, the E-R diagram for the situation would include no crow's feet. This situation is illustrated in Figure 2.2.

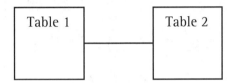

Figure 2.2 *One-to-One Entity Relationship Diagram*

The relationship between two tables in a one-to-one relationship would be captured by embedding the primary key of one of the tables as a foreign key in the other table. Keeping the relationship one-to-one becomes a data entry, or integrity, requirement. Each primary key value can appear only once as a foreign key value.

2.4 The Role-to-Actor Relationship: Not One-to-Many

In the example database, one actor can play many roles, but one role cannot be played by many actors. Two movies may have roles with the same name, which represent the same character. In such a situation, those roles are given different roleID values, and they are distinct. For example, more than one Batman movie has been made, and the role of Batman is included in each movie. Table 2.3, the Role table, contains separate rows with different roleID values for each of the different Batman roles.

TABLE 2.3 Role

roleID	roleName	gender	actorID
00095	Batman	M	00076
00097	The Joker	M	00019
00106	Batman	M	00080

In some cases, the same role—with the character at different ages or in different guises—may appear in the same movie and be played by one or more actors. Once again, those roles are given different roleID values, and they are distinct. Consider the Role table in Table 2.4. In the movie *Forrest Gump,* there are two different Forrest Gump roles, which were played by different actors.

TABLE 2.4 Role

roleID	roleName	gender	actorID
00057	Forrest Gump	M	00001
00062	Young Forrest Gump	M	00033

2.5 The Number of Entities Participating in Relationships

Naming relationships as "one-to-many" and "one-to-one" is actually a simplification. Consider the values in Table 2.5, the Actor table, and Table 2.6, the Role table. Information is given in the Actor table for three actors, but there are no roles containing their actorIDs. There is nothing wrong with having actors without roles in the database. Perhaps you have recorded information about the actors without having recorded information about their roles yet.

Information is given in the Role table for three roles, but there are no actors who played these roles. The practical effect is that the actorID field in the Role table is null. There is nothing wrong with having roles without actors in the database. Perhaps you would like to record information about these roles even when the actor is unknown.

TABLE 2.5 Actor

actorID	lastName	firstName	birthDate
00001	Hanks	Tom	7/9/1956
00002	Paxton	Bill	5/17/1955
00003	Bacon	Kevin	7/8/1958

TABLE 2.6 Role

roleID	roleName	gender	actorID
00095	Batman	M	
00097	The Joker	M	
00106	Batman	M	

The design of the Actor and Role tables is capable of supporting one-to-one or one-to-many relationships, but the data in the tables do not exhibit either one of these relationships. Even though phrases like "one-to-many" are used to describe relationships, a more precise definition of a situation might use a phrase like "one-to-zero or more," for example. The common name of a type of relationship between tables might indicate that there is one row in the relationship. This name doesn't rule out the possibility of zero rows, however. Similarly, the name might indicate that there are many rows in the relationship, which doesn't rule out the possibility of one or zero rows.

2.6   The Referential Integrity Constraint

If two tables are in a primary key to foreign key relationship, the foreign key values in the table that contains them can be said to refer to the corresponding primary key values in the other table. This structure imposes an important constraint on the correctness of data stored in the tables, known as referential integrity. Tables 2.7 and 2.8 illustrate this idea. These Actor and Role tables contain an instance of *incorrect* data. The information in the Role table is correct for the roles Colonel Nathan R. Jessep and the Joker; however, the information on Batman is not correct. Batman is shown as being played by actorID 00076, but no such actorID appears in the Actor table. The foreign key value in the Role table refers to a value that doesn't exist in the primary key table—a violation of referential integrity. The referential integrity constraint can be stated in two ways:

1. Every foreign key value has to appear as a primary key value.
2. There can be no foreign key value that does not appear as a primary key value.

TABLE 2.7 Actor

actorID	lastName	firstName
00019	Nicholson	Jack

TABLE 2.8 Role

roleID	roleName	gender	actorID
00052	Colonel Nathan R. Jessep	M	00019
00095	Batman	M	00076
00097	The Joker	M	00019

The importance of referential integrity cannot be overemphasized. It makes no sense to create an actorID value in the Role table that refers to an actor who doesn't exist in the Actor table. Practically speaking, violations of referential integrity are errors for the same reason that violations of data integrity are errors: They mislead users into thinking they are retrieving useful information when, in fact, they are not.

An actorID pulled out of thin air violates referential integrity, but a null value does not. If the actor who played Batman is not known or has not been recorded yet, then the actorID for that role should be null. Tables 2.9 and 2.10 show Actor and Role tables containing values that have no referential integrity problem. The actor for the Batman role does not exist in the Actor table, so the actorID value for Batman in the Role table is null.

TABLE 2.9 Actor

actorID	lastName	firstName
00019	Nicholson	Jack

TABLE 2.10 Role

roleID	roleName	gender	actorID
00052	Colonel Nathan R. Jessep	M	00019
00095	Batman	M	
00097	The Joker	M	00019

2.7 The Many-to-Many Relationship

There is a many-to-many relationship between actors and movies. Each actor can play various roles in different movies, and each movie can have various roles played by various actors. This many-to-many relationship can be captured by expanding the Role table to include the movieID column. Tables 2.11, 2.12, and 2.13 contain the Actor, Role, and Movie tables, respectively, with sample data illustrating this idea.

TABLE 2.11 Actor

actorID	lastName	firstName	birthDate
00001	Hanks	Tom	7/9/1956
00032	Field	Sally	11/6/1946

TABLE 2.12 Role

roleID	roleName	actorID	movieID
00057	Forrest Gump	00001	007
00061	Mrs. Gump	00032	007
00063	Jim Lovell	00001	001

TABLE 2.13 Movie

movieID	title	year	company
001	Apollo 13	1995	Imagine Entertainment and Universal Pictures
007	Forrest Gump	1994	Steve Tisch/Wendy Finerman

As the tables show, a one-to-many relationship exists between actors and roles. The data in the Actor and Role tables show that Tom Hanks played the role Forrest Gump in the movie *Forrest Gump* and the role Jim Lovell in the movie *Apollo 13*. A one-to-many relationship also exists between movies and roles. The data in the Movie and Role tables show that the movie *Forrest Gump* had two roles, Forrest Gump and Mrs. Gump, played by Tom Hanks and Sally Field, respectively. A many-to-many relationship is captured by two one-to-many relationships. In total, three tables are required, with a table in the middle between the two tables in the many-to-many relationship. In this example, the Role table is the table in the middle. It has the columns actorID and movieID embedded in it as foreign keys; these columns are the primary keys of the Actor and Movie tables.

The E-R diagram in Figure 2.3 shows the relationships among the three tables in an easily understandable way.

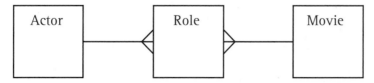

Figure 2.3 *Actor-Role-Movie Entity Relationship Diagram*

2.8 The Example Database Expanded and Concatenated Primary Keys

A database on the motion picture industry could potentially include many different tables. In addition to information on actors, movies, and roles, the example database for this book includes information on memorable movie quotes. Each role in a movie may have more than one quote, and a quote may be spoken by more than one role. In other words, a many-to-many relationship exists between roles and quotes. RoleQuote is the table in the middle, which captures the many-to-many relationship.

Tables 2.14, 2.15, and 2.16 contain the Role, RoleQuote, and Quote tables, respectively, with sample data illustrating this idea. In the movie *The Wizard of Oz*, Dorothy says the lines, "Toto, I've got a feeling we're not in Kansas anymore." and "There's no place like home." Dorothy, the Scarecrow, and the Tin Man all say the line, "Lions and tigers and bears, oh my!" The one-to-many relationship between Role and RoleQuote is reflected by the fact that roleID 00001 appears three times in the RoleQuote table. The one-to-many relationship between Quote and RoleQuote is reflected by the fact that quoteID 0033 appears three times in the RoleQuote table.

TABLE 2.14 Role

roleID	roleName	actorID
00001	Dorothy Gale	00061
00003	The Scarecrow	00063
00005	The Tin Man	00065

TABLE 2.15 RoleQuote

roleID	quoteID
00001	0031
00001	0033
00001	0036
00003	0033
00005	0033

TABLE 2.16 Quote

quoteID	quoteText
0031	Toto, I have a feeling we're not in Kansas anymore.
0033	Lions and tigers and bears, oh my!
0036	There's no place like home.

Table 2.15, the RoleQuote table, illustrates an additional idea. It contains no columns other than the foreign keys roleID and quoteID. Each matchup of role and quote is unique, so these two columns together can serve as the primary key of the table. It is not necessary to create a separate primary key column. When the values in more than one column together uniquely identify a row and when these columns are used as the primary key, they are collectively known as a concatenated primary key.

2.9 The Complete Example Database

The E-R diagram in Figure 2.4 shows the design of the complete example database with the relationships discussed previously among the Actor, Movie, Role, Quote, and RoleQuote tables.

The small tables used in the foregoing illustrations have given some idea of the contents of the example database. The complete schema for each of the tables is given next. These schemas are very close in form to the SQL syntax for defining and creating tables, which will be explained in Chapter 6. Because of this similarity, the data types and key notations are given in uppercase letters, as they will be in Chapter 6. Each schema is followed by explanatory comments for each column in the table.

Actor

(actorID	TEXT(5)	PRIMARY KEY,
lastName	TEXT(24),	
firstName	TEXT(24),	
middleName	TEXT(24),	
suffix	TEXT(6),	
gender	TEXT(1),	
birthDate	DATE,	
deathDate	DATE)	

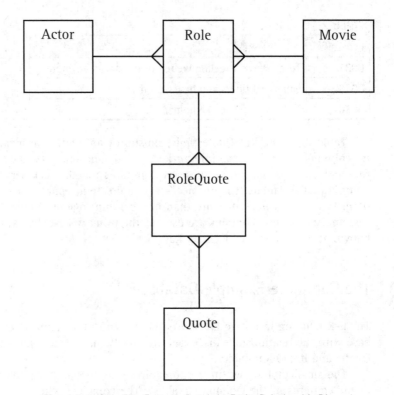

Figure 2.4 *Complete Example Database Entity Relationship Diagram*

actorID: This column contains the unique identifier for an actor.

lastName: This column contains the last name of the actor's stage name.

firstName: This column contains the first name of the actor's stage name.

middleName: This column contains the middle name, middle initial, or anything else commonly given between the first and last names of the actor's stage name.

suffix: This column contains name suffixes, such as "Jr."

gender: This column contains the actor's gender.

birthDate: This column contains the actor's date of birth, if it's known.

deathDate: This column contains the actor's date of death, if there is one and it's known.

Movie

(movieID	TEXT(3)	PRIMARY KEY,
title	TEXT(36),	
year	NUMBER,	
company	TEXT(50),	
totalNoms	NUMBER,	
awardsWon	NUMBER,	
DVDPrice	CURRENCY,	
discountPrice	CURRENCY)	

movieID: This column contains the unique identifier for a movie.

title: This column contains the title of the movie.

year: This column contains the year when the movie was released.

company: This column contains the name of the production company that produced the movie.

totalNoms: This column contains the total number of Academy Awards for which the movie was officially nominated.

awardsWon: This column contains the number of Academy Awards won by the movie.

DVDPrice: This column contains a representative retail price for a DVD of the movie (as of 2008).

discountPrice: This column contains a representative discount price for a DVD of the movie (as of 2008).

Role

(roleID	TEXT(5)	PRIMARY KEY,
roleName	TEXT(36),	
gender	TEXT(1),	
actorID	TEXT(5)	FOREIGN KEY,
movieID	TEXT(3)	FOREIGN KEY)

roleID: This column contains the unique identifier for a role.

roleName: This column contains the name of a role.

gender: This column contains the gender of a role.

actorID: This column is a foreign key referring to the primary key of the Actor table; it gives the actor who played the role.

movieID: This column is a foreign key referring to the primary key of the Movie table; it gives the movie the role was in.

Quote

(quoteID	TEXT(4)	PRIMARY KEY,
quoteText	TEXT(255))	

quoteID: This column contains the unique identifier for a quote.

quoteText: This column contains the text of a quote by one or more characters in a movie.

RoleQuote

(roleID	TEXT(5)	PRIMARY KEY, FOREIGN KEY,
quoteID	TEXT(4)	PRIMARY KEY, FOREIGN KEY)

roleID: This column is part of the concatenated primary key of this table. It is a foreign key referring to the primary key of the Role table; it gives the role that spoke the quote.

quoteID: This column is part of the concatenated primary key of this table. It is a foreign key referring to the primary key of the Quote table; it gives the quote that was spoken.

2.10 Data for the Example Database

The example database contains information on 24 movies, 100 actors, 138 roles, and 43 quotes. The RoleQuote table has 45 rows. For the movies listed, not all of the roles, actors, or possible quotes are included. Even though this is obviously just a small subset of all motion picture information, because of the large number of rows and columns in each table, it is not practical to show the complete contents in printed form here. If you download the database, it should be a simple matter to display the complete contents when working with it. There is a worthwhile insight here: By definition, the benefits of a database management system become apparent as soon as a data set grows to the size where it's inconvenient to manage the data in printed form. At the same time, it may be helpful to print out copies of the tables and refer to them when reading the rest of the chapters and working the problems in this book.

Queries in SQL

3.1   What Is SQL?

SQL is an acronym that stands for Structured Query Language. SQL is an international standard, and all fully relational database management systems include it. Using SQL, it is possible to create a database, enter data into it, and retrieve information from it. Any information that can be retrieved from a database can be retrieved by means of an SQL query.

Most database management systems also have a graphical user interface (GUI). Using this GUI, it's possible to create a database and enter data into a database. Using a feature known as query by example (QBE), it is possible to retrieve information from a database. A query language like SQL is a more powerful and flexible means of querying a database, however, so this book covers only SQL.

The ultimate goal of maintaining a database is to retrieve useful information from it. This book emphasizes querying databases and only briefly covers database creation (in Chapter 6). Because this book is so short, only the most basic and important query features of SQL are covered.

To write SQL queries, you need to know the keywords and syntax of the language. Keywords are words that have a special meaning when used in a query. A query is made up of keywords, the names of tables and columns in the database, and attribute values. The syntax describes the rules for arranging the parts of a query.

This book presents SQL features by means of specific examples. In general, keywords and syntax are explained briefly; the intent of a query is described in English; the corresponding SQL query is given; and, where practical, the data retrieved by the query are shown. At the end of each chapter, problems similar to the examples allow you to practice using the syntax and generalize from the examples given. Both the example queries and solutions to the problems are provided in the example database.

The queries in this book are written using certain conventions intended to make them easier to read. SQL is not case sensitive, and the conventions for capitalization of table and column names used in Chapters 1 and 2 are continued. The keywords in queries will be given in all uppercase letters. It doesn't matter whether an SQL query is written on a single line or broken into several lines. Example queries will typically be broken into separate lines corresponding to the keywords used. SQL queries end with a semicolon. If you forget the semicolon in Microsoft Access, the SQL editor will supply one.

3.2 Simple SQL Queries and the Keywords SELECT and FROM

The two most basic keywords in SQL are SELECT and FROM. SQL also contains the wildcard symbol, the asterisk (*). This symbol can be used to stand for the list of all columns in a table. The simplest query in SQL takes this form:

```
SELECT *
FROM TableName;
```

The results of running such a query are the complete contents of the specified table. Example Query 3-1 is a concrete example of such a query.

Example Query 3-1
```
SELECT *
FROM Role;
```

The output of Example Query 3-1 would start as shown in the Example Query 3-1 Results. The table contains 138 rows, so it's not practical to show the complete results here.

Example Query 3-1 Results

roleID	roleName	gender	actorID	movieID
00001	Dorothy Gale	F	00061	016
00002	The Wizard of Oz	M	00062	016
00003	The Scarecrow	M	00063	016
...	...	...	...	...

3.3 Projection

Projection is the technical term that describes choosing to include only some of the columns in the results of a query. It is easy to accomplish this task by replacing the * symbol after the SELECT keyword in a query with a list of the desired columns in the table, separated by commas. For example, if you wanted to see all of the rows of the Role table, but only the columns roleID, roleName, and gender for each row, you could write Example Query 3-2.

Example Query 3-2

```
SELECT roleID, roleName, gender
FROM Role;
```

The output of Example Query 3-2 would start as shown in the Example Query 3-2 Results.

Example Query 3-2 Results

roleID	roleName	gender
00001	Dorothy Gale	F
00002	The Wizard of Oz	M
00003	The Scarecrow	M
. . .	. . .	. . .

3.4 Column Aliases and the Keyword AS

Column names in table designs can't have spaces in them, and it is helpful if they're short—which explains the use of column names such as roleID. A column alias is an alternative name that can be displayed in the results of a query, making it more user friendly. (An alias is a substitute name for something.) To create aliases, you use the keyword AS plus square brackets, which serve as a kind of quotation mark. Example Query 3-3 illustrates this practice.

Example Query 3-3

```
SELECT roleID AS [role identifier], roleName AS [role name],
gender
FROM Role;
```

The output of Example Query 3-3 would start as shown in the Example Query 3-3 Results. In the results, the column headings contain the phrases given in brackets in the query instead of the names of the table columns.

Example Query 3-3 Results

role identifier	role name	gender
00001	Dorothy Gale	F
00002	The Wizard of Oz	M
00003	The Scarecrow	M
. . .	. . .	. . .

3.5   Selection on Text Columns and the Keyword WHERE

Selection is the technical term that describes choosing to include only some of the rows in the results of a query. The keyword that makes this kind of selectivity possible is WHERE. It follows the FROM keyword and uses the operators for equality and inequality: <, <=, =, >=, and >. In SQL, the following pair of symbols stands for "not equals": <>. Selection is usually accomplished by comparing a given value with the contents of a particular column. Only those rows that meet the condition applied to the column are included in the results. If the comparison value is text, then it must be enclosed in single quotes.

Suppose you wanted to find the roleID, roleName, and gender for those roles in the movie with movieID equal to '014'. This query is applied to the Role table. Although movieID is the primary key of the Movie table, it also appears in the Role table as a foreign key. You are making a condition on the movieID column, but it is not necessary to include this column in the results. The movieID value in the query has to appear in single quotes because movieID is a text column. Example Query 3-4 illustrates this.

Example Query 3-4

```
SELECT roleID, roleName, gender
FROM Role
WHERE movieID = '014';
```

The complete output of Example Query 3-4 is shown in Example Query 3-4 Results.

Example Query 3-4 Results

roleID	roleName	gender
00037	The Terminator	M
00038	Kyle Reese	M
00039	Sarah Connor	F

3.6 Selection on Number Columns

The WHERE keyword works in the same way for number columns as it does for text columns. The inequality operators work for text columns, but they are more commonly used for number columns. When you use a numeric value in a query, that value cannot contain any commas and can contain at most one decimal point. Otherwise, the value can consist of only digits.

Suppose you wanted to find the movieID, title, year, and totalNoms of all movies that received more than 10 Academy Award nominations. Example Query 3-5 shows this query.

Example Query 3-5

```
SELECT movieID, title, year, totalNoms
FROM Movie
WHERE totalNoms > 10;
```

The complete output of Example Query 3-5 is shown in the Example Query 3-5 Results.

Example Query 3-5 Results

movieID	title	year	totalNoms
007	Forrest Gump	1994	13
009	Gone with the Wind	1939	15
024	Amadeus	1984	11

3.7 Selection on Currency Columns

Currency columns are displayed with dollar ($) signs and two decimal places, but in queries they work just like regular number columns. When comparing a currency column with a numeric value in the query, the numeric value cannot contain a dollar sign or any commas and can contain at most one decimal point. Otherwise, it can consist of only digits.

Suppose you wanted to find the movieID, title, year, DVDPrice, and discountPrice of all movies where the discountPrice is greater than or equal to $24.99. Example Query 3-6 shows this query.

Example Query 3-6

```
SELECT movieID, title, year, DVDPrice, discountPrice
FROM Movie
WHERE discountPrice >= 24.99;
```

The complete output of Example Query 3-6 is shown in the Example Query 3-6 Results.

Example Query 3-6 Results

movieID	title	year	DVDPrice	discountPrice
011	Naked City, The	1948	$29.99	$29.99
019	Batman	1989	$26.99	$24.99
020	Batman Returns	1992	$26.99	$24.99
021	Batman Forever	1995	$26.99	$24.99

3.8 Selection on Date Columns

A date value can be given in mm/dd/yy or mm/dd/yyyy form, using digits for the month, day, and year values. If desired, you can use dashes as separators instead of slashes. Dates are composite data types, consisting of three parts. Each of the individual parts is numeric in nature. Dates have a property in common with text fields: They have to be enclosed in punctuation marks. This practice prevents the slashes or dashes used as separators in them from being interpreted as arithmetic operations. A date value can be enclosed in # signs rather than single quotes. The # signs serve as a reminder that dates have a numeric aspect.

Suppose you wanted to find the actorID, lastName, firstName, middleName, suffix, and birthDate of all actors who were born before January 1, 1885. Example Query 3-7 shows this query.

Example Query 3-7

```
SELECT actorID, lastName, firstName, middleName, suffix,
birthDate
FROM Actor
WHERE birthDate < #1/1/1885#;
```

The complete output of Example Query 3-7 is shown in the Example Query 3-7 Results.

Example Query 3-7 Results

actorID	lastName	firstName	middleName	suffix	birthDate
00068	Blandick	Clara			6/4/1880
00012	Greenstreet	Sydney			12/27/1879
00096	Grapewin	Charley			12/20/1869

3.9 Selection with NULL, IS, and NOT

NULL is a keyword that signifies a column contains no value for a given row. The keyword NULL is not a value, so it should not be enclosed in quotes. When checking to see whether a column contains NULL, instead of using the equality operator, (=), you use the keyword IS.

Every person is born on some date, but not all of the actors have birthdates recorded for them in the Actor table. Suppose you wanted to find the actorID, lastName, firstName, middleName, and suffix of all actors whose birthDate is null. Example Query 3-8 shows this query.

Example Query 3-8

```
SELECT actorID, lastName, firstName, middleName, suffix
FROM Actor
WHERE birthDate IS NULL;
```

The complete output of Example Query 3-8 is shown in the Example Query 3-8 Results.

Example Query 3-8 Results

actorID	lastName	firstName	middleName	suffix
00033	Humphreys	Michael	Conner	
00069		Terry		

If you want to test for inequality with NULL, you need to use the keyword IS with the keyword NOT. Suppose you wanted to find the actorID, lastName, firstName, middleName, and suffix of all actors whose suffix is not null. Example Query 3-9 shows this query.

Example Query 3-9

```
SELECT actorID, lastName, firstName, middleName, suffix
FROM Actor
WHERE suffix IS NOT NULL;
```

The complete output of Example Query 3-9 is shown in the Example Query 3-9 Results.

Example Query 3-9 Results

actorID	lastName	firstName	middleName	suffix
00047	Gooding	Cuba		jr.

3.10 Queries with the Keyword LIKE

Quite often with text fields the user does not have a perfect recollection of the value or values of interest. If a query is written using the = sign, results will be returned only on an exact match. It is possible to write more flexible queries using the keyword LIKE along with the wildcard symbol, *. In this usage, the * represents any sequence of characters that can appear in a text column. A value for comparison is formed by mixing * with actual letters, digits, and so forth, and enclosing the result in single quotes. For example, when used with the keyword LIKE, the value 'Batman*' would match with any movie title that started with the word "Batman." It is important to note that LIKE is used in place of the = sign and does not require the keyword IS. If you wrote a query containing IS LIKE, it would not work.

Suppose you wanted to find the movieID and title of the movies where the title starts with "Batman." Example Query 3-10 shows this query.

Example Query 3-10

```
SELECT movieID, title
FROM Movie
WHERE title LIKE 'Batman*';
```

The complete output of Example Query 3-10 is shown in the Example Query 3-10 Results.

Example Query 3-10 Results

movieID	title
019	Batman
020	Batman Returns
021	Batman Forever
022	Batman & Robin
023	Batman Begins

3.11 The Logical Operators AND and OR

More than one condition can be included after the WHERE in a query by combining the conditions with the keywords AND or OR. If conditions are combined with AND, each one of the conditions has to be true for the combination to be true. If conditions are combined with OR, if one or both of the conditions are true, then the combination is true. Both AND and OR can be applied to conditions that are placed on the same column or on different columns. If there are two conditions on the same column, each of the conditions has to be complete; they cannot be shortened. For example, you can write WHERE X < 3 OR X > 5, but you cannot write WHERE X < 3 OR > 5. It is also incorrect to use WHERE more than once, so you cannot write WHERE X < 3 OR WHERE X > 5.

Suppose you wanted to find the actorID, lastName, firstName, middleName, suffix, and birthDate of all female actors who were born after January 1, 1975. The two conditions that you want to hold true are the facts that the actor is female and that the actor was born after January 1, 1975. This case is an example of a query using AND where the two conditions are applied to two different columns. Example Query 3-11 shows this query.

Example Query 3-11

```
SELECT actorID, lastName, firstName, middleName, suffix,
birthDate
FROM Actor
WHERE gender = 'F'
AND birthDate > #1/1/1975#;
```

The complete output of Example Query 3-11 is shown in the Example Query 3-11 Results.

Example Query 3-11 Results

actorID	lastName	firstName	middleName	suffix	birthDate
00025	Hoffman	Gaby			1/8/1982
00085	Barrymore	Drew			2/22/1975
00089	Silverstone	Alicia			10/4/1976
00094	Holmes	Katie			12/18/1978

Suppose you'd like to find the movieID, title, DVDPrice, and discountPrice of all movies where the DVDPrice is either less than $10.00 or greater than $27.00. This case is an example of a query using OR where the two conditions are applied to the same column. Example Query 3-12 shows this query.

Example Query 3-12

```
SELECT movieID, title, DVDPrice, discountPrice
FROM Movie
WHERE DVDPrice < 10.00
OR DVDPrice > 27.00;
```

The complete output of Example Query 3-12 is shown in the Example Query 3-12 Results.

Example Query 3-12 Results

movieID	title	DVDPrice	discountPrice
011	Naked City, The	$29.99	$29.99
013	Sudden Impact	$9.99	$9.99
015	Terminator 2: Judgment Day	$9.99	$7.99

It is possible to create arbitrarily complex WHERE conditions by using AND, OR, NOT, and parentheses to group expressions.

3.12 Problem Queries

Write SQL statements that accomplish the following:

3-1. Find all columns and rows of the Actor table.

3-2. Find all columns and rows of the Movie table.

3-3. Find the movieID, title, and year of all movies.

3-4. Find the quoteText of all quotes.

3-5. Find the actorID, lastName, firstName, middleName, and suffix of all actors. The actorID, lastName, firstName, and middleName column headings should have spaces in them: actor ID, last name, first name, middle name.

3-6. Find the movieID, title, DVDPrice, and discountPrice of all movies. The column headings should have spaces in them: movie ID, DVD price, discount price.

3-7. Find the actorID, lastName, firstName, middleName, and suffix of all female actors.

3-8. Find the movieID, title, and year of all movies where the production company was Warner Brothers.

3-9. Find the movieID, title, and year of all movies that were nominated for no Academy Awards.

3-10. Find the movieID, title, year, totalNoms, and awardsWon of all movies that won more than five Academy Awards.

3-11. Find the movieID, title, year, and DVDPrice of all movies where the DVD-Price is $9.99.

3-12. Find the movieID, title, year, and DVDPrice of all movies where the DVD-Price is equal to the discountPrice.

3-13. Find the actorID, lastName, firstName, middleName, suffix, and deathDate of all actors who died after January 1, 1980.

3-14. Find the actorID, birthDate, and deathDate for any actors whose date of death is before their date of birth. If the data in the database are correct, this query should give no results.

3-15. Find the actorID, lastName, firstName, middleName, suffix, and birthDate of all actors whose deathDate is NULL.

3-16. Find the actorID, lastName, firstName, middleName, and suffix of all actors whose middleName is NOT NULL.

3-17. Suppose you remember a movie quote as "Play it again, Sam." However, when you write a query to find this quote, you get no results. Write a query that will find the text of all movie quotes that begin with the word "Play."

3-18. Suppose you remember the role of Joker in one of the Batman movies, but when you write a query to find this role, you get no results. Write a query that will find the roleID and roleName of any role where Joker appears as part of the role name.

3-19. Find the movieID, title, year, and totalNoms of all movies that were nominated for more than five Academy Awards and were released before 1950.

3-20. Find the movieID, title, year, and awardsWon of all movies that either won more than five Academy Awards or were released after 1990.

3-21. Find the movieID, title, year, and discountPrice of all movies with discount prices between $15.00 and $20.00, inclusive.

3-22. Find the actorID, lastName, firstName, middleName, and suffix of all actors who are dead males.

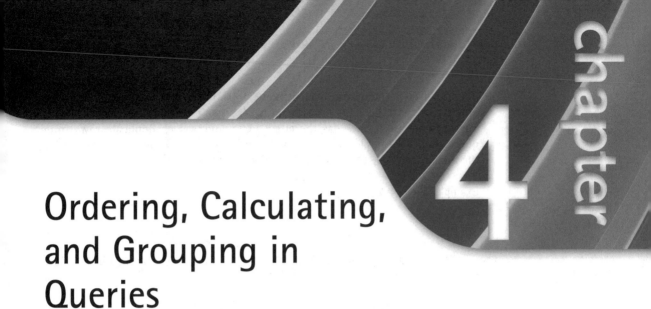

Ordering, Calculating, and Grouping in Queries

4.1 The Keyword DISTINCT

Not only is the information retrieved from a database important, but how the results are presented to users is also important. Although tables themselves are not allowed to have duplicate rows, query results can easily contain duplicates. Suppose you ran Example Query 4-1.

Example Query 4-1

```
SELECT roleID
FROM RoleQuote;
```

The output of Example Query 4-1 would start as shown in the Example Query 4-1 Results. There would be as many rows in the results as appear in the RoleQuote table. Because individual roles can have more than one quote, the query results would include duplicate roleID values.

Example Query 4-1 Results

roleID
00001
00001
00001
00002
00003
. . .

If a user is interested in identifying only those roles that had quotes, the duplication in the results is not helpful: You can't see the forest for the trees. The keyword DISTINCT has the effect of removing such duplicate rows from query results. Example Query 4-2 is the same as Example Query 4-1 except for the inclusion of DISTINCT after the keyword SELECT.

Example Query 4-2

```
SELECT DISTINCT roleID
FROM RoleQuote;
```

The output of Example Query 4-2 would start as shown in the Example Query 4-2 Results.

Example Query 4-2 Results

roleID
00001
00002
00003
00005
00007
. . .

The keyword DISTINCT can also be used when the query selects more than one column. In such a query, DISTINCT comes before the list of columns and does not require parentheses or other punctuation. In this situation, rows are considered to be duplicates if they contain the same complete set of column values. DISTINCT has the effect of leaving only one row with a given set of values in it and removing any duplicate rows from the query results.

4.2 The Keywords ORDER BY

Presenting query results in a particular order can be very helpful to users. For example, a user might want to see rows of query results alphabetized by one of the text columns in it or arranged in ascending or descending order by one of the number columns in it. In other words, it might be desirable to see query results in sorted order. SQL does not have a keyword "alphabetize" or "sort." Instead, presenting query results in sorted order is accomplished with the keywords ORDER BY. These keywords appear at the end of the query, along with the name of the column to sort on.

Suppose you wanted to find the movieID and title of all movies in the Movie table, in order by title. Example Query 4-3 shows this query.

Example Query 4-3

```
SELECT movieID, title
FROM Movie
ORDER BY title;
```

The output of Example Query 4-3 would start as shown in the Example Query 4-3 Results.

Example Query 4-3 Results

movieID	title
024	Amadeus
001	Apollo 13
019	Batman
022	Batman & Robin
. . .	. . .

The movie *A Few Good Men* is in the database, but it is listed as "Few Good Men, A." Example Query 4-3 illustrates why: If the movie title were given with the article "A" first, it would appear in the results of the query along with the other movie titles starting with the letter "A."

4.3 The Keywords ASC and DESC

When ordering results, the default is to sort them in ascending order. If you want to make this order explicit, you put the keyword ASC after the name of the column you're ordering on. If you would like results to appear in descending order, use the keyword DESC instead. Example Query 4-4 illustrates the use of this keyword.

Example Query 4-4

```
SELECT movieID, title
FROM Movie
ORDER BY title DESC;
```

The output of Example Query 4-4 would start as shown in the Example Query 4-4 Results.

Example Query 4-4 Results

movieID	title
016	Wizard of Oz, The
017	Tootsie
014	Terminator, The
015	Terminator 2: Judgment Day
. . .	. . .

Example Query 4-4 again illustrates the usefulness of removing an article from the beginning of a movie title and putting it at the end. If *The Wizard of Oz* were listed with "The" first, "Tootsie" would appear at the top of the results and "The Wizard of Oz" would come second.

4.4 Ordering on More Than One Column

It is possible to order the results of a query on more than one column. The columns of interest are given after the keywords ORDER BY, separated by commas. The results are ordered first by the first column given, then by the next column given, and so on. It is possible to mix ascending and descending order by putting one of the ASC and DESC keywords after the names of the columns. The default is ascending order.

Suppose you wanted to find the actorID, lastName, and firstName of all actors, ordered first by lastName and then by firstName. In other words, you wanted the actors' names alphabetized, last name first. To keep the query manageable, middleName and suffix are not included in the ordering, although they would need to be included in a complete example. Example Query 4-5 shows this query.

Example Query 4-5
```
SELECT actorID, lastName, firstName
FROM Actor
ORDER BY lastName, firstName;
```

Partial output of Example Query 4-5 is given in the Example Query 4-5 Results. This output includes some of the rows where actors have the same last name, showing that overall, rows are ordered by lastName, and rows with the same lastName value are ordered by firstName.

Example Query 4-5 Results

actorID	lastName	firstName
00069		Terry
00098	Abraham	F.
00003	Bacon	Kevin
. . .	. . .	. . .
00058	Hamilton	Linda
00067	Hamilton	Margaret
. . .	. . .	. . .
00070	Hoffman	Dustin
00025	Hoffman	Gaby
. . .	. . .	. . .

Notice the lastName column of the very first row; it is null. When presenting the results in order, the null value comes first. Null is treated as "less than" any actual value.

4.5 Calculated Columns in Results

It can be convenient to have query results showing the results of calculations on number columns in tables. Arithmetic expressions can be built out of the names of number columns, numeric constants, addition, subtraction, multiplication, division, and parentheses. The symbols +, -, *, and / are used for addition, subtraction, multiplication, and division, respectively.

Suppose you wanted to find the movieID, title, DVDPrice, and discountPrice of movies, along with the difference between the regular DVDPrice and the discountPrice. DVDPrice and discountPrice are both currency columns, so the difference can be found by subtracting the one price column from the other. Example Query 4-6 shows this query.

Example Query 4-6

```
SELECT movieID, title, DVDPrice, discountPrice,
DVDPrice - discountPrice
FROM Movie;
```

The output of Example Query 4-6 would start as shown in the Example Query 4-6 Results.

Example Query 4-6 Results

movieID	title	DVDPrice	discountPrice	Expr1004
001	Apollo 13	$12.99	$9.99	$3.00
002	Casablanca	$19.99	$14.99	$5.00
003	Dirty Harry	$16.99	$16.99	$0.00
. . .	. . .	. . .	. . .	. . .

Notice that the system makes up an arbitrary expression name for the calculated column in the results. This is a good place to use the keyword AS and create a more informative column name. The next example does so and also illustrates a more complicated arithmetic expression.

Suppose these conditions apply when buying or renting a movie:

1. You estimate that if you buy a movie outright, on average you watch it four times. Also, if you buy a movie, you buy it at the discount price.

2. You estimate that the total cost to you of renting a movie is $3.00. This may include gas money if you go to a video store, the value of the time spent searching online if you use such a service, and so on.

Now suppose that you wanted to find the movieID and title of a movie, along with the difference between the average cost of viewing it if bought at the discount price and the cost of viewing it if rented. This difference is the actual additional cost per viewing if you add the movie to your collection. Let the calculated column have the heading "cost per viewing if bought." Example Query 4-7 shows the query you need.

Example Query 4-7

```
SELECT movieID, title, (discountPrice / 4) - 3 AS [cost per
viewing if bought]
FROM Movie;
```

The output of Example Query 4-7 would start as shown in the Example Query 4-7 Results.

Example Query 4-7 Results

movieID	title	cost per viewing if bought
001	Apollo 13	-0.5025
002	Casablanca	0.7475
003	Dirty Harry	1.2475
. . .	. . .	. . .

It is apparent from Example Query 4-7 that if you bought *Apollo 13,* you would save money. If you bought *Casablanca* or *Dirty Harry,* you would lose money. Of course, after seeing the results, you might conclude that you would watch these movies more than the average number of times, and it would pay off to buy them anyway.

4.6   The Date Functions YEAR, MONTH, and DAY

SQL also includes a number of built-in functions. The date data type illustrates the kind of function that computes or extracts a value from a column for each row included in the query. The names of the functions that apply to dates are YEAR, MONTH, and DAY. In a query, these keywords are followed by parentheses containing the name of a date column. The functions extract that part of the date for which they are named.

Suppose you wanted to find the actorID, lastName, and year of birth of all actors. Example Query 4-8 shows this query.

Example Query 4-8

```
SELECT actorID, lastName, YEAR(birthDate)
FROM Actor;
```

The output of Example Query 4-8 would start as shown in the Example Query 4-8 Results.

Example Query 4-8 Results

actorID	lastName	Expr1002
00001	Hanks	1956
00002	Paxton	1955
00003	Bacon	1958
. . .	. . .	. . .

Because the component parts of dates have a numeric nature, it is possible to do arithmetic on them. You can subtract dates directly, although you will get results that you may not expect. Suppose you wanted to find the actorID, last-Name, and the difference between the deathDate and the birthDate of all actors where the deathDate is not null. Example Query 4-9 shows this query.

Example Query 4-9

```
SELECT actorID, lastName, deathDate - birthDate
FROM Actor
WHERE deathDate IS NOT NULL;
```

The output of Example Query 4-9 would start as shown in the Example Query 4-9 Results.

Example Query 4-9 Results

actorID	lastName	Expr1002
00008	Bergman	25202
00068	Blandick	29899
00007	Bogart	21175
. . .	. . .	. . .

The difference between deathDate and birthDate is an unexpectedly large number because it is expressed in days instead of years. If you wanted to find the difference in years, you could rewrite the query using the YEAR function. Example Query 4-10 shows the new query.

Example Query 4-10

```
SELECT actorID, lastName, YEAR(deathDate) - YEAR(birthDate)
FROM Actor
WHERE deathDate IS NOT NULL;
```

The output of Example Query 4-10 would start as shown in the Example Query 4-10 Results.

Example Query 4-10 Results

actorID	lastName	Expr1002
00008	Bergman	69
00068	Blandick	82
00007	Bogart	58
. . .	. . .	. . .

Although the results in years are convenient for review purposes, Example Query 4-10 is not entirely precise. It does not take into account whether the month and day of a person's death fall before or after the month and day of that individual's birth. The results shown may be off by a year. It would be necessary to write yet another query to solve this problem.

4.7 The Built-In Function COUNT

The keyword COUNT is a built-in function that makes it possible to find the number of rows that would be retrieved by a query with a given set of conditions. Suppose you wanted to find the number of rows in the Actor table. Example Query 4-11 shows this query.

Example Query 4-11

```
SELECT COUNT(*)
FROM Actor;
```

The complete output of Example Query 4-11 is shown in the Example Query 4-11 Results.

Example Query 4-11 Results

Expr1000
100

The count is a single number, so the results of Example Query 4-11 are a table consisting of a single row and a single column. The column heading is an arbitrary expression unless the keyword AS is used in the query to define a specific heading.

In Query 4-11, the wildcard symbol * does not signify "count all rows." Rather, it signifies that when doing the count, all columns are taken into consideration. A row will be included in the count as long as at least one of the columns contained in it is not null. All rows should meet this condition, and there is no WHERE condition restricting the number of rows included in the query results, so all rows in the table are counted.

Suppose you wanted to find the number of actors whose last names start with the letter "S." Example Query 4-12 shows this query.

Example Query 4-12

```
SELECT COUNT(*)
FROM Actor
WHERE lastName LIKE 'S*';
```

The complete output of Example Query 4-12 is shown in the Example Query 4-12 Results. Example Query 4-12 counts the number of rows in the Actor table that meets the condition following the WHERE.

Example Query 4-12 Results

Expr1000
6

The keyword COUNT can also be applied to one or more listed columns rather than to *. COUNT will return a count of all rows where those columns are not null. Suppose you'd like to find the number of actors for whom one column, lastName, is not null. Example Query 4-13 shows this query.

Example Query 4-13

```
SELECT COUNT(lastName)
FROM Actor;
```

The complete output of Example Query 4-13 is shown in the Example Query 4-13 Results.

Example Query 4-13 Results

Expr1000
99

Notice that it would be redundant to include the condition WHERE lastName IS NOT NULL in Example Query 4-13.

4.8 The Built-In Functions MAX, MIN, SUM, and AVG

The MAX, MIN, SUM, and AVG keywords refer to the mathematical concepts of maximum, minimum, sum, and average, respectively. These keywords are the names of built-in functions that can be applied to number columns in tables. To use one of these functions, you put the number column of interest in parentheses after the function name. These functions give values that are based on the contents of more than one row in a table.

Suppose you wanted to find the average DVDPrice of all movies in the Movie table. Example Query 4-14 shows this query.

Example Query 4-14

```
SELECT AVG(DVDPrice)
FROM Movie;
```

The complete output of Example Query 4-14 is shown in the Example Query 4-14 Results.

Example Query 4-14 Results

Expr1000
$17.99

Suppose you wanted to find the sum of the discountPrice values of all movies in the Movie table. Example Query 4-15 shows this query.

Example Query 4-15

```
SELECT SUM(discountPrice)
FROM Movie;
```

The complete output of Example Query 4-15 is shown in the Example Query 4-15 Results.

Example Query 4-15 Results

Expr1000
$361.76

As you saw earlier, calculated columns may be defined using built-in functions such as the date functions, because those functions extract a single value for each row in the query. However, built-in functions such as AVG, which group together values of more than one row, do not mix with arithmetic calculations in some implementations of SQL.

For example, suppose you wanted to find the difference between the DVD-Price of each movie and the average DVDPrice of all of the movies. Example Query 4-16 illustrates this idea.

Example Query 4-16

```
SELECT DVDPrice - AVG(DVDPrice)
FROM Movie;
```

Unfortunately, depending on the system you are using, this query might not work. This example is saved as Example Query 4-16 in this book's Microsoft Access database, but trying to run it will generate an error message rather than results.

4.9   The Keywords GROUP BY

Grouping is a powerful capability in SQL. It allows you to generate query results that summarize table information in a way that is similar to a report. Grouping is based on SQL's built-in functions that aggregate the information found in tables.

Grouping has similarities to ordering in its logic. The general plan of a query using GROUP BY is this: From a given table, the query selects a column of interest, column X, for example. The query also selects one of the built-in functions, COUNT, for example. At the end of the query, the keywords GROUP BY are followed by the name of the column of interest, X. Different values for column X may occur more than once in the table. This GROUP BY query will count how many times each different value of X occurs.

In the Movie table, each movie appears only once; however, different movies are produced by the same company, so the companies may appear more than once in the table. Suppose you wanted find out how many movies each company produced. In other words, you want to count how many times each company appears in the Movie table. Example Query 4-17 shows this query.

Example Query 4-17

```
SELECT company, COUNT(*)
FROM Movie
GROUP BY company;
```

The output of Example Query 4-17 would end as shown in the Example Query 4-17 Results. The expression column contains the counts.

Example Query 4-17 Results

company	Expr1001
. . .	. . .
Steve Tisch/Wendy Finerman	1
The Malpaso Company	2
TriStar Pictures	1
Warner Brothers	6

Now suppose instead that you wanted to find the average DVDPrice grouped by company. Example Query 4-18 shows this query.

Example Query 4-18

```
SELECT company, AVG(DVDPrice)
FROM Movie
GROUP BY company;
```

The output of Example Query 4-18 would end as shown in the Example Query 4-18 Results. The expression column contains the averages.

Example Query 4-18 Results

company	Expr1001
. . .	. . .
Steve Tisch/Wendy Finerman	$14.99
The Malpaso Company	$13.49
TriStar Pictures	$14.99
Warner Brothers	$22.66

A GROUP BY query has to contain a built-in function that aggregates values from different rows. The SELECT operation can include only what you're grouping on and the built-in function. Technically, the SELECT expression doesn't have to include the grouping column—but without it, the meaning of the results may not be clear.

4.10   GROUP BY **and** ORDER BY

GROUP BY and ORDER BY can be used in the same query. In the previous example, the query results happened to be ordered by company. You can change the order of the results if you like—for example, ordering them by the value of the results of the built-in function.

Suppose you wanted to find the average DVDPrice grouped by company, presented in ascending order by the average DVDPrice. Example Query 4-19 illustrates this.

Example Query 4-19

```
SELECT company, AVG(DVDPrice)
FROM Movie
GROUP BY company
ORDER BY AVG(DVDPrice);
```

The output of Example Query 4-19 would start as shown in the Example Query 4-19 Results.

Example Query 4-19 Results

company	Expr1001
CarolCo Pictures	$9.99
Imagine Entertainment and Universal Pictures	$12.99
Gordon Company	$12.99
The Malpaso Company	$13.49
. . .	. . .

4.11 The Keyword HAVING

In a simple query, you can limit the number of rows in the results by using the keyword WHERE, which puts a condition on one or more of the columns of the table. In a GROUP BY query, you can use the keyword HAVING to put a condition on those values of the built-in function that will be included in the results. HAVING appears at the end of the query and can use a constant value and the comparison operators (<, <=, =, >=, >, and <>).

Running the previous query would have produced results that included all companies and the average values of their DVDPrice. To save space, only partial results were shown. Suppose, however, that you wanted to see just the results for those companies where the average DVDPrice is less than or equal to $14.00. Example Query 4-20 illustrates this idea.

Example Query 4-20

```
SELECT company, AVG(DVDPrice)
FROM Movie
GROUP BY company HAVING AVG(DVDPrice) <= 14.00
ORDER BY AVG(DVDPrice);
```

The complete output of Example Query 4-20 is shown in the Example Query 4-20 Results.

Example Query 4-20 Results

company	Expr1001
CarolCo Pictures	$9.99
Gordon Company	$12.99
Imagine Entertainment and Universal Pictures	$12.99
The Malpaso Company	$13.49

4.12 Grouping by More Than One Column

Just as it's possible to order by more than one column at a time, it's also possible to group by more than one column at a time. The different grouping columns are included in the SELECT expression, followed by the built-in function. The different grouping columns are also included after the keywords GROUP BY, separated by commas. Every different combination of values in the grouping columns will give a separate row in the results.

In the example database, different movies might have the same DVDPrice. Among those movies with the same DVDPrice, there may be different values for the discountPrice. Suppose you wanted to find the number of movie DVDs grouped by their DVDPrice and their discountPrice. Example Query 4-21 shows this query.

Example Query 4-21

```
SELECT DVDPrice, discountPrice, COUNT(*)
FROM Movie
GROUP BY DVDPrice, discountPrice;
```

The output of Example Query 4-21 would start as shown in the Example Query 4-21 Results.

Example Query 4-21 Results

DVDPrice	discountPrice	Expr1002
$9.99	$7.99	1
$9.99	$9.99	1
$12.99	$9.99	2
$14.99	$9.99	7
$14.99	$14.99	2
. . .	. . .	. . .

The last two lines of the Example Query 4-21 Results table illustrate the idea of multiple groups most clearly. There are two groups of movies where the DVDPrice is $14.99. The first group consists of seven movies with a DVDPrice of $14.99 and a discountPrice of $9.99. The second group consists of two movies with a DVDPrice of $14.99 and a discountPrice of $14.99.

4.13 Problem Queries

Write SQL statements that accomplish the following:

4-1. Find the distinct actorID values that occur in the Role table.

4-2. Find the distinct companies that occur in the Movie table.

4-3. Find the actorID, lastName, firstName, middleName, and suffix of all actors. Order the results by the lastName column. Notice that the value NULL for lastName sorts before any actual value.

4-4. Find the quoteID and quoteText of all quotes. Order the results (alphabetically) by the quoteText.

4-5. Find the movieID, title, and totalNoms of all movies. Order the results in descending order by totalNoms.

4-6. Find the movieID, title, and DVDPrice of all movies. Order the results in descending order by DVDPrice.

4-7. Find the movieID, title, totalNoms, and awardsWon of all movies. Order the results by totalNoms and awardsWon.

4-8. Find the movieID, title, DVDPrice, and discountPrice of all movies. Order the results by DVDPrice and discountPrice.

4-9. Find the movieID, title, and year of all movies, along with the difference between totalNoms and awardsWon. For the column heading of the calculated column, use "nominated but not won."

4-10. Suppose you have a special membership at a store that qualifies you for 10% off all of your purchases, including discount prices. Find the movieID, title, and year of all movies, along with the discount price minus 10% of the discount price. For the column heading of the calculated column, use "my price."

4-11. Find the actorID, lastName, and month of birth of all actors.

4-12. Find the actorID, lastName, and year of death of all actors where the death-Date column is not null.

4-13. Find the count of the number of quotes in the Quote table.

4-14. Find the count of the number of middle names that occur in the Actor table.

4-15. Find the maximum value of totalNoms occurring in the Movie table.

4-16. Find the average number of awardsWon in the Movie table.

4-17. Find the gender and the count (of all rows of that gender) in the Actor table, grouped by gender.

4-18. Find the year and the sum of awardsWon in the Movie table, grouped by year.

4-19. Find the year and the sum of awardsWon in the Movie table, grouped by year and ordered by the sum of the awardsWon.

4-20. Find the totalNoms and the maximum number of awardsWon in the Movie table, grouped by totalNoms and ordered by the maximum number of awardsWon.

4-21. Find the roleID and the count of quotes in the RoleQuote table, grouped by roleID, having a count greater than or equal to 3.

4-22. Find the movieID and the count of roleIDs in the Role table, grouped by movieID, having the count of roles greater than 6.

4-23. Find the movieID, gender, and count of all columns in the Role table, grouped by movieID and gender.

4-24. Find the company, year, and sum of awardsWon for movies, grouped by company and year.

chapter 5

Complex Queries and Join Queries

5.1   Selection Queries with DISTINCT

Chapter 3 covered basic SQL queries using the keywords SELECT and WHERE. Chapter 4 introduced ordering, calculating, and grouping in queries. To keep the presentation of the new material in Chapter 4 straightforward, the examples did not include some of the features that had been introduced earlier in Chapter 3. Not all features of SQL can be combined in the same query, but the majority can. For example, you can easily use the keyword DISTINCT when writing a query that uses WHERE.

Suppose you wanted to find the distinct discountPrice values of movies that have won Academy Awards. Example Query 5-1 shows this query.

Example Query 5-1

```
SELECT DISTINCT discountPrice
FROM Movie
WHERE awardsWon <> 0;
```

The complete output of Example Query 5-1 is shown in the Example Query 5-1 Results.

Example Query 5-1 Results

discountPrice
$7.99
$9.99
$14.99
$17.99
$22.99
$24.99
$29.99

5.2 Selection Queries with Calculated Columns and DISTINCT

Calculated columns can be used in queries containing the keyword WHERE, and DISTINCT can be used with calculated columns. For example, suppose you wanted to find the distinct differences between the DVDPrice and the discount-Price of movies that have won Academy Awards. Example Query 5-2 shows this query.

Example Query 5-2

```
SELECT DISTINCT DVDPrice - discountPrice
FROM Movie
WHERE awardsWon <> 0;
```

The complete output of Example Query 5-2 is shown in the Example Query 5-2 Results.

Example Query 5-2 Results

Expr1000
$0.00
$2.00
$3.00
$5.00

5.3 Selection Queries with GROUP BY

GROUP BY can also be used in queries containing the keyword WHERE. For example, suppose you wanted to find the movieID and the count of the roleID values in it for female roles only, grouped by movieID. In other words, suppose you wanted to find how many female roles were recorded in the database for each movie. Example Query 5-3 shows this query.

Example Query 5-3

```
SELECT movieID, COUNT(roleID)
FROM Role
WHERE gender = 'F'
GROUP BY movieID;
```

A representative subset of the output of Example Query 5-3 is shown in the Example Query 5-3 Results.

Example Query 5-3 Results

movieID	Expr1001
. . .	. . .
016	6
017	3
018	2
019	1
. . .	. . .

5.4 The Join and Qualified Column Names

In a correctly designed database, for every kind of entity there is a separate table, and the information about one instance of the entity is stored in a row of the table. The information in a database consists of both the information stored in individual tables and the relationships between entries in different tables. Take actors and roles, for example. One actor can play many roles. The actorID exists as a primary key in the Actor table and as a foreign key in the Role table. The presence of the actorID column in both tables forms a primary key to foreign key relationship. This relationship between the columns in the tables captures the relationship between the actor and role entities stored in the tables.

Table 5.1 contains a subset of the Actor table, and Table 5.2 contains a subset of the Role table. Tom Hanks' actorID, 00001, appears twice as a foreign key value in the subset of the Role table. From these occurrences, you can determine that Tom Hanks played the roles of Forrest Gump and Jim Lovell. Gary Sinise's actorID, 00004, appears once as a foreign key value in the subset of the Role table. From this occurrence, you can determine that Gary Sinise played the role of Lieutenant Dan Taylor.

TABLE 5.1 Actor

actorID	lastName	firstName	middleName	suffix	gender	birthDate	deathDate
00001	Hanks	Tom			M	7/9/1956	
00002	Paxton	Bill			M	5/17/1955	
00003	Bacon	Kevin			M	7/8/1958	
00004	Sinise	Gary			M	3/17/1955	
. . .	. . .	. . .			. . .	. . .	. . .

TABLE 5.2 Role

roleID	roleName	gender	actorID	movieID
. . .	. . .	. . .	. . .	. . .
00057	Forrest Gump	M	00001	007
00058	Jenny Curran	F	00030	007
00059	Lieutenant Dan Taylor	M	00004	007
00060	Private Benjamin Buford "Bubba" Blue	M	00031	007
00061	Mrs. Gump	F	00032	007
00062	Young Forrest Gump	M	00033	007
00063	Jim Lovell	M	00001	001
. . .	. . .	. . .	. . .	. . .

Every example query up to this point has retrieved information from just one table. In SQL, however, you can also retrieve information from more than one related table at a time. The word "join" is used to describe this kind of query. SQL has several alternative ways of forming join queries—but note that the way shown here does *not* use a keyword named "JOIN."

The relationships between entities may be one-to-one, one-to-many, or many-to-many. For any pair of tables that form a relationship, the primary key of the *one* table is embedded as a foreign key in the *many* table. The presence of the primary key of one table as a foreign key in another is the basis for a join query. This query is structured to find matches between the corresponding columns in the two tables. With the Actor and Role tables, for example, you would be interested in finding the rows in the Actor table with a given actorID and finding the rows in the Role table that have a matching value of actorID.

Suppose you wanted to write an SQL query to these specifications: Each row in the results would contain the complete information for one of the actors, followed by the complete information for one of the roles the actor played. Altogether there would be one row in the results for each role. Because an actor can play more than one role, the information for an actor could appear in more than one row of the results. Example Query 5-4 illustrates this idea. Explanations of the syntax will follow.

Example Query 5-4

```
SELECT *
FROM Actor, Role
WHERE Actor.actorID = Role.actorID;
```

Line by line, this is what you find in Example Query 5-4:

1. The SELECT expression is not unusual. The * symbol is used to keep the query uncomplicated. The Actor table has 8 columns, and the Role table has 5 columns. Thus, the results would have 13 columns. This is too many columns to show conveniently on the printed page, so the results of this query are not provided here. If desired, the results can be viewed by running Example Query 5-4 in the example database.

2. The two tables involved in the join are listed following the FROM keyword, separated by a comma. If a query involves more than one table, each one has to be included in this way.

3. The join is defined after the WHERE keyword. This is where the corresponding columns of the two tables are given. The condition Actor.actorID = Role.actorID specifies that the rows of interest in the two tables are those rows where the actorID values are the same. Because the columns of interest in the two tables have the same name, the columns' names must be qualified by the name of the table in which they appear. Dot notation is used for this purpose.

5.5 The Join with Projection

Projection refers to the idea that you might want to see only a limited number of columns in the results of a query. It is very useful for join queries, which can lead to a very large number of columns in the results.

Suppose you wanted to find the actorID, lastName, firstName, roleID, and roleName of all rows of the Actor and Role tables that matched on actorID. It is necessary to use qualified column names in two places in this query, in the joining condition and in the SELECT expression. The need for dot notation in the joining condition was explained in the previous example. The need for dot notation in the SELECT expression is similar. When joining the Actor and Role tables, you could specify either Actor.actorID or Role.actorID in the SELECT expression because the value retrieved by either would be the same; however, you have to use one or the other, and not just the actorID. Whenever a column name is used in a query and more than one table in the query has a column with that name, you must qualify the name using dot notation.

Example Query 5-5 illustrates a join with projection.

Example Query 5-5

```
SELECT Actor.actorID, lastName, firstName, roleID, roleName
FROM Actor, Role
WHERE Actor.actorID = Role.actorID;
```

The output of Example Query 5-5 would start as shown in the Example Query 5-5 Results.

Example Query 5-5 Results

actorID	lastName	firstName	roleID	roleName
00001	Hanks	Tom	00057	Forrest Gump
00001	Hanks	Tom	00063	Jim Lovell
00002	Paxton	Bill	00064	Fred Haise
00003	Bacon	Kevin	00054	Captain Jack Ross
00003	Bacon	Kevin	00065	Jack Swigert
. . .	. . .	. . .	. . .	. . .

5.6 The Cartesian Product

The term "Cartesian product" refers to a situation where each row in one table is matched with each row in another table, regardless of the column values they contain. The Cartesian product is of theoretical importance, but it is rarely of practical use. If you are trying to write a join query and you forget to include the WHERE keyword and the joining condition, the result will be a Cartesian product. This is one of the easiest mistakes to make.

Consider Example Query 5-6. There are 100 actors in the Actor table and 138 roles in the Role table. Example Query 5-6 says to match each actor with each role, regardless of whether the actor played the role. There are 100 times 138 rows (13,800 rows) in the complete results. When you create a Cartesian product by accident, you will typically recognize your mistake by the number of rows in the result. The fact that the number of rows in the result is the arithmetic product of the numbers of rows in the two tables is a reminder of why this result is known as a product.

Example Query 5-6

```
SELECT Actor.actorID, lastName, firstName, roleID, roleName
FROM Actor, Role;
```

A representative subset of the output of the Cartesian product is shown in the Example Query 5-6 Results. Every actor is matched with the role Dorothy Gale. Buried in this list is Judy Garland, the actor who actually played that role.

Example Query 5-6 Results

actorID	lastName	firstName	roleID	roleName
. . .	. . .	. . .	. . .	. . .
00059	Furlong	Edward	00001	Dorothy Gale
00046	Gable	Clark	00001	Dorothy Gale
00061	Garland	Judy	00001	Dorothy Gale
00029	Getz	John	00001	Dorothy Gale
00027	Goldblum	Jeff	00001	Dorothy Gale
. . .	. . .	. . .	. . .	. . .

5.7 Joins with Additional WHERE Conditions

The idea of complex queries involving multiple parts was introduced in the previous sections. Some of the most useful queries are those that join two tables and include WHERE conditions on one or more columns of either of the two tables involved. Suppose you wanted to find the actorID, lastName, firstName, roleID, and roleName for Jack Nicholson only. Such a query would join the Actor and Role tables. It would also have a condition on the Actor table, which would be included with the keyword AND. Example Query 5-7 illustrates this idea.

Example Query 5-7

```
SELECT Actor.actorID, lastName, firstName, roleID, roleName
FROM Actor, Role
WHERE Actor.actorID = Role.actorID
AND lastName = 'Nicholson' AND firstName = 'Jack';
```

The complete output of Example Query 5-7 is shown in the Example Query 5-7 Results.

Example Query 5-7 Results

actorID	lastName	firstName	roleID	roleName
00019	Nicholson	Jack	00052	Colonel Nathan R. Jessep
00019	Nicholson	Jack	00097	The Joker
00019	Nicholson	Jack	00098	Jack Napier

It is possible to create an interesting example of a join query that includes a condition testing for inequality between columns of the two joined tables. Suppose you wanted to find the actorID, lastName, actor's gender, roleID, roleName, and role's gender for those cases where the gender of the actor and the gender of the role were not the same. Example Query 5-8 illustrates this idea. Note that dot notation must be used to distinguish the two columns named "gender."

Example Query 5-8

```
SELECT Actor.actorID, lastName, Actor.gender, roleID,
roleName, Role.gender
FROM Actor, Role
WHERE Actor.actorID = Role.actorID
AND Actor.gender <> Role.gender;
```

The complete output of Example Query 5-8 is shown in the Example Query 5-8 Results.

Example Query 5-8 Results

actorID	lastName	Actor.gender	roleID	roleName	Role.gender
00070	Hoffman	M	00078	Dorothy Michaels (Tootsie)	F
00073	Williams	M	00082	Mrs. Doubtfire	F

5.8 Joins with ORDER BY

Just as simple selection queries can be combined with ordering, grouping, and calculating, so, too, can join queries be combined with these features. For example, ORDER BY can be used with a join.

Suppose you wanted to find the movieID, lastName, firstName, roleID, and roleName for all actors and roles, ordered by movieID and lastName. Notice that movieID comes from the Role table, whereas lastName comes from the Actor table. The join is formed on the two tables Role and Actor, and the ordering of the results depends on the columns taken from each of these two tables. Example Query 5-9 illustrates this idea.

Example Query 5-9

```
SELECT movieID, lastName, firstName, roleID, roleName
FROM Actor, Role
WHERE Actor.actorID = Role.actorID
ORDER BY movieID, lastName;
```

The output of Example Query 5-9 would start as shown in the Example Query 5-9 Results.

Example Query 5-9 Results

movieID	lastName	firstName	roleID	roleName
001	Bacon	Kevin	00065	Jack Swigert
001	Hanks	Tom	00063	Jim Lovell
001	Harris	Ed	00067	Gene Kranz
001	Paxton	Bill	00064	Fred Haise
001	Quinlan	Kathleen	00068	Marilyn Lovell
001	Sinise	Gary	00066	Ken Mattingly
002	Bergman	Ingrid	00017	Ilsa Lund (Laszlo)
002	Bogart	Humphrey	00016	Rick Blaine
002	Greenstreet	Sydney	00021	Signor Ferrari
002	Henreid	Paul	00018	Victor Laszlo
002	Lorre	Peter	00022	Ugarte
002	Rains	Claude	00019	Captain Renault
...	...	...	...	...

5.9 Joins with GROUP BY and HAVING

GROUP BY and HAVING can be combined with a join query. For example, suppose you wanted to find the titles of movies, along with the number of roles in them, grouped by title and having at least five roles. The titles come from the Movie table, whereas the number of roles depends on the count of the rows in the Role table with matching values for movieID. This query graphically illustrates the idea of a one-to-many relationship. Grouping is done on the *one* table, Movie, and counting is done on the *many* table, Role. HAVING restricts the results to those movies with at least five roles. Example Query 5-10 illustrates this idea.

Example Query 5-10
```
SELECT title, COUNT(roleID)
FROM Movie, Role
WHERE Movie.movieID = Role.movieID
GROUP BY title HAVING COUNT(roleID) >= 5;
```

The output of Example Query 5-10 would start as shown in the Example Query 5-10 Results.

Example Query 5-10 Results

title	Expr1001
Apollo 13	6
Batman	5
Batman & Robin	11
. . .	. . .

Example Query 5-10 is the kind of query where it can be easy to forget the joining condition because you are so involved in arranging the grouping and conducting the count; however, you would immediately recognize that you had made a mistake when you looked at the results of the query without a joining condition.

5.10 Three-Way and Multi-Way Joins

In the example database, a many-to-many relationship exists between the Actor table and the Movie table. This relationship is captured by embedding the primary key of the Actor table as a foreign key in the Role table and by embedding the primary key of the Movie table as a foreign key in the Role table.

The Role table is the table in the middle in this many-to-many relationship. It is quite possible that someone might want to retrieve information that comes from related rows in all three of these tables.

Suppose you wanted to find the actorID and lastName from the Actor table, the roleID and roleName from the Role table, and the movieID and title from the Movie table. The critical point is that you would want the actor to match the role played, and you would want the role to match the movie in which it appeared. This query would require joining the Actor and Role tables on the actorID column and simultaneously joining the Role and Movie tables on the movieID column. Thus, the query must include two joining conditions, as shown in Example Query 5-11.

Example Query 5-11

```
SELECT Actor.actorID, lastName, roleID, roleName,
Movie.movieID, title
FROM Actor, Role, Movie
WHERE Actor.actorID = Role.actorID
AND Role.movieID = Movie.movieID;
```

The output of Example Query 5-11 would start as shown in the Example Query 5-11 Results.

Example Query 5-11 Results

actorID	lastName	roleID	roleName	movieID	title
00061	Garland	00001	Dorothy Gale	016	Wizard of Oz, The
00062	Morgan	00002	The Wizard of Oz	016	Wizard of Oz, The
00063	Bolger	00003	The Scarecrow	016	Wizard of Oz, The
. . .	. . .	. . .	. . .	. . .	. . .

The example database contains five tables overall. By definition, because they appear in the same database, they are all related to one another in some way. The relationships between the Actor, Role, and Movie tables were reviewed earlier. In addition, a many-to-many relationship exists between the Role table and the Quote table. This is captured by embedding the primary key of the Role table as a foreign key in the RoleQuote table and by embedding the primary key of the Quote table as a foreign key in the RoleQuote table. The previous example query—a three-way join—had three tables and two joining conditions in it. In general, a query with more than three tables and two joins in it is known as a multi-way join. An example can be formed by writing a query that depends on the relationships among all five tables of the example database.

Suppose you wanted to find the lastName of the actor, the roleName, the title of the movie, and the quoteText of the quote spoken for all actors, roles, movies, and quotes in the database. Writing this query involves all five tables, and it requires four joining conditions, one for each pairing of tables in a relationship. Example Query 5-12 shows this query.

Example Query 5-12

```
SELECT lastName, roleName, title, quoteText
FROM Actor, Role, Movie, RoleQuote, Quote
WHERE Actor.actorID = Role.actorID
AND Role.movieID = Movie.movieID
AND Role.roleID = RoleQuote.roleID
AND RoleQuote.quoteID = Quote.quoteID;
```

The output of Example Query 5-12 would start as shown in the Example Query 5-12 Results.

Example Query 5-12 Results

lastName	roleName	title	quoteText
Garland	Dorothy Gale	Wizard of Oz, The	Toto, I have a feeling we're not in Kansas anymore.
Garland	Dorothy Gale	Wizard of Oz, The	Lions and tigers and bears, oh my!
Garland	Dorothy Gale	Wizard of Oz, The	There's no place like home.
Morgan	The Wizard of Oz	Wizard of Oz, The	Pay no attention to that man behind the curtain!
Bolger	The Scarecrow	Wizard of Oz, The	Lions and tigers and bears, oh my!
. . .	. . .	. . .	. . .

Three-way and multi-way join queries could also be made more complex by the inclusion of the other features illustrated earlier. Results could be counted, ordered, grouped, and otherwise manipulated.

5.11 Joins with Calculated Columns and Built-In Functions

In this section, the use of built-in functions and calculated columns is illustrated with join queries. Recall that the Movie and Role tables are in a one-to-many relationship, with the primary key of the Movie table, movieID, embedded as a foreign key in the Role table. Suppose you wanted to find the sum of the discountPrice values of all movies in which Batman appears as a role. You have to join the two tables on movieID. The discountPrice column in the SELECT expression comes from the Movie table, whereas the roleName column in the WHERE expression comes from the Role table. Example Query 5-13 illustrates this idea.

Example Query 5-13
```
SELECT SUM(discountPrice)
FROM Movie, Role
WHERE Movie.movieID = Role.movieID
AND roleName = 'Batman';
```

The complete output of Example Query 5-13 is shown in the Example Query 5-13 Results.

Example Query 5-13 Results

Expr1000
$100.95

It is possible to create an interesting example of a three-way join query that includes a calculated column with a built-in date function. Suppose you wanted to find the actorID and lastName, the movieID and title, and the age of the actor when the movie was made. To match the actors and the movies, it is necessary to join them through the Role table, and extract the year from the actor's birthDate, then subtract that year from the year the movie was made. Example Query 5-14 shows the resulting query.

Example Query 5-14
```
SELECT Actor.actorID, lastName, Movie.movieID, title,
year - YEAR(birthDate)
FROM Actor, Role, Movie
WHERE Actor.actorID = Role.actorID
AND Role.movieID = Movie.movieID;
```

The output of Example Query 5-14 would start as shown in the Example Query 5-14 Results.

Example Query 5-14 Results

actorID	lastName	movieID	title	Expr1004
00061	Garland	016	Wizard of Oz, The	17
00062	Morgan	016	Wizard of Oz, The	49
00063	Bolger	016	Wizard of Oz, The	35
...	...	...	...	...

Because movies have years instead of dates, it is possible that the calculated age value is off by one. Whether this error occurs depends on whether the actor's date of birth came before or after the release date of the movie—but this information can't be determined from the data in the database.

5.12 Subqueries

Because a query returns a set of results in tabular form, in principle, wherever a table occurs in a query, it is possible to substitute a query for that table. You can write a single SQL query that consists of a combination of two queries, one of which is the outer, main query, and the other of which is the inner, subquery. The subquery plays the role of a table in the outer query.

As pointed out earlier, depending on the version of SQL, Example Query 5-15 may not find the difference between DVDPrice and the average DVDPrice; however, using a subquery, it is possible to generate the desired results. As shown in Example Query 5-16, the subquery is enclosed in parentheses. In the subquery, you would find the average DVDPrice for all of the rows in the Movie table. It is important to use the keyword AS to give this result column its own name. The outer query then finds the difference between the DVDPrice column of the Movie table and the named result column of the inner query. In effect, the outer query involves two tables; however, it is not necessary to have a joining condition in the query overall because there is only one value in the results of the inner query.

Example Query 5-15
```
SELECT DVDPrice - AVG(DVDPrice)
FROM Movie;
```

Example Query 5-16
```
SELECT DVDPrice - avgDVDPrice
FROM Movie,
  (SELECT AVG(DVDPrice) AS avgDVDPrice
   FROM Movie);
```

The output of Example Query 5-16 would start as shown in the Example Query 5-16 Results. Depending on the system you're using, the results of Example Query 5-16 may show negative currency values in parentheses—a convention from the accounting world.

Example Query 5-16 Results

Expr1000
($5.00)
$2.00
($1.00)
. . .

Another aspect of the example should also be noted. If you are using Microsoft Access, you can enter the query as shown previously, and it will work correctly. If you save the query, however, the next time you open it with the Access SQL editor, it will be given in this much less understandable form:

```
SELECT DVDPrice - avgDVDPrice
FROM Movie, [SELECT AVG(DVDPrice) AS avgDVDPrice
   FROM Movie]. AS [%$##[at]_Alias];
```

A query is given below, which shows the use of DISTINCT nested inside the parentheses of the COUNT function. This syntax does not work in Microsoft Access, and it is not possible to save a query containing this error. For this reason, this example query is unnumbered and does not exist in the example database.

Example Query 5-x.
```
SELECT COUNT(DISTINCT lastName)
FROM Actor;
```

Using a subquery, however, it becomes possible to generate the desired results. The subquery is enclosed in parentheses, as shown in Example Query 5-17. In the inner query, you find the distinct values of lastName in the Actor table. The outer query then counts the number of rows in the results of the inner query.

Example Query 5-17
```
SELECT COUNT(*)
FROM
  (SELECT DISTINCT lastName
  FROM Actor);
```

The complete output of Example Query 5-17 is shown in the Example Query 5-17 Results.

Example Query 5-17 Results

Expr1000
95

If you did a query with COUNT(lastName), no null values would be counted, but duplicates would. With Example Query 5-17, duplicates are not counted, but COUNT(*) means that the count of 95 includes one distinct last-Name value which happens to be null.

If you are using Microsoft Access, you can enter the query as shown earlier, and it will work correctly. If you save the query, however, the next time you open it with the Access SQL editor, it will be given in this much less understandable form:

```
SELECT COUNT(*)
FROM [SELECT DISTINCT lastName
    FROM Actor]. AS [%$#[at]_Alias];
```

SQL has many query features. The most basic and useful ones were covered in Chapters 3 through 5 of this book. Using these features, you can write queries that satisfy the vast majority of the requests for information retrieval from a database. If you decide you want to go further in the study of databases, what you have learned while working through these chapters should provide a solid foundation for learning more advanced and powerful aspects of SQL.

5.13 Problem Queries

Write SQL statements that accomplish the following:

5-1. Find the distinct awards won by movies with discount prices of $9.99.

5-2. Find the actorID, lastName, firstName, middleName, suffix, and birthDate of rows in the Actor table where the gender is F. Order the results by the actor's date of birth.

5-3. Find the movieID, title, year, DVDPrice, and half of the DVDPrice (the price for a half-off sale) of movies that have a DVDPrice greater than or equal to $20.00.

5-4. Find the sum of the discount prices of movies made after 1979.

5-5. Find the awards won and the average discount price of movies made before 1980, grouped by awards won.

5-6. Find the awards won and the maximum discount price of movies made after 1979, grouped by awards won, having a maximum discount price greater than $9.99.

5-7. Find all columns of the join between the Movie and Role tables where the value of movieID is the same in both.

5-8. Find all columns of the join between the Quote and RoleQuote tables where the value of quoteID is the same in both.

5-9. Find the movieID, title, and year, and the roleID and roleName in the join between the Movie and Role tables where the value of movieID is the same in both.

5-10. Find the roleID, quoteID, and quoteID in the join between the Quote and RoleQuote tables where the value of quoteID is the same in both.

5-11. Find all columns of the Cartesian product of the Movie and Role tables.

5-12. Find all columns of the Cartesian product of the Quote and RoleQuote tables.

5-13. Find the movieID, title, and year of movies, and the roleID and roleName of roles for the join of the Movie and Role tables where the gender of the role is female.

5-14. Find the roleID, quoteID, and quoteText in the join between the Quote and RoleQuote tables where the roleID is 00001 or 00003.

5-15. Find the movieID, title, and year of movies and the roleID and roleName of roles in the join of the Movie and Role tables. Order the results by the movieID.

5-16. Find the roleID, quoteID, and quoteText in the join between the Quote and RoleQuote tables. Order the results by the roleID and quoteID.

5-17. Find the movie title and the number of roleIDs associated with it, grouped by movie title, having a count of six or more roles.

5-18. Find the roleName and the number of quoteIDs associated with it, grouped by roleName, having at least two quotes per roleName.

5-19. Find the lastName, firstName, middleName, and suffix of actors matched with the quoteID spoken by those actors.

5-20. Find the title and year of movies matched with the quoteID spoken in that movie.

5-21. Find the maximum DVDPrice for a movie with a role played by actorID 00001.

5-22. Find the distinct actorID and lastName, the movie ID and title, and the number of years that the actor lived after the movie was made for those actors with a deathDate in the Actor table. It seems a little odd, but notice that Mark Hellinger died the year before the release of the movie *The Naked City*. Just as with the birthDate example in Section 5.12, because movies have years instead of dates, the difference in years between a date of death and a movie may be off by one.

5-23. Find the difference between the maximum DVDPrice of all movies and the DVDPrice of each individual movie.

5-24. Find the count of the distinct years of movies in the database.

Creating Tables and Entering Data

6.1 Graphical User Interface Alternatives and SQL

Using SQL for querying is important—even for the beginner—because of SQL's power and flexibility. Using SQL, it is also possible to create tables, insert data into them, update data in them, and delete data from them. These operations can be carried out through the graphical user interface (GUI) of systems such as Microsoft Access. For the beginner, using the graphical user interface for these purposes is intuitive and straightforward. In other words, for simple tasks, using a GUI is easier than using SQL. This book does not cover any of the details specific to Microsoft Access. If the reader wants to experiment with the GUI in Access, Microsoft's Help and other resources are available, and it is not difficult to become familiar with the GUI.

This book also does not cover all of the aspects of SQL. Nevertheless, it strives to be complete in the following sense: If you want to create and use the example database using only SQL, everything necessary to do so is explained. You can download the complete database from the Jones and Bartlett web page for this book. Alternatively, you could create the database from scratch. How to do so using SQL is explained in the following sections.

6.2 The Keywords CREATE TABLE

At the end of Chapter 2, schemas were given that defined the tables in the example database. The SQL keywords CREATE TABLE, when combined with such a definition, form a special kind of query that can be run just like the queries of the previous chapters. Such a query creates a table rather than retrieving data from a table.

Example Queries 6-1 through 6-5 contain the CREATE TABLE statement for each of the tables in the example database. These queries include the SQL syntax for specifying primary and foreign keys. That syntax is explained in Section 6.3.

Example Query 6-1

```
CREATE TABLE Actor
(actorID TEXT(5),
lastName TEXT(24),
firstName TEXT(24),
middleName TEXT(24),
suffix TEXT(6),
gender TEXT(1),
birthDate DATE,
deathDate DATE,
CONSTRAINT ActorPK PRIMARY KEY (actorID));
```

Example Query 6-2

```
CREATE TABLE Movie
(movieID TEXT(3),
title TEXT(36),
year NUMBER,
company TEXT(50),
totalNoms NUMBER,
awardsWon NUMBER,
DVDPrice CURRENCY,
discountPrice CURRENCY,
CONSTRAINT MoviePK PRIMARY KEY (movieID));
```

Example Query 6-3

```
CREATE TABLE Quote
(quoteID TEXT(4),
quoteText TEXT(255),
CONSTRAINT QuotePK PRIMARY KEY (quoteID));
```

Example Query 6-4

```
CREATE TABLE Role
(roleID TEXT(5),
roleName TEXT(36),
gender TEXT(1),
actorID TEXT(5),
```

```
movieID TEXT(3),
CONSTRAINT RolePK PRIMARY KEY (roleID),
CONSTRAINT ActorFK FOREIGN KEY (actorID) REFERENCES Actor
  (actorID),
CONSTRAINT MovieFK FOREIGN KEY (movieID) REFERENCES Movie
  (movieID));
```

Example Query 6-5

```
CREATE TABLE RoleQuote
(roleID TEXT(5),
quoteID TEXT(4),
CONSTRAINT RoleQuotePK PRIMARY KEY (roleID, quoteID),
CONSTRAINT RoleFK FOREIGN KEY (roleID) REFERENCES Role
  (roleID),
CONSTRAINT QuoteFK FOREIGN KEY (quoteID) REFERENCES Quote
  (quoteID));
```

6.3 Constraints and the Keywords CONSTRAINT, PRIMARY KEY, FOREIGN KEY, and REFERENCES

Specifying keys in tables imposes constraints on which data the key columns can contain. In SQL, keys can be defined as instances of constraints on the table. The last line of the definition of the Actor table in Example Query 6-1 is representative of how a primary key can be defined:

```
CONSTRAINT ActorPK PRIMARY KEY (actorID)
```

To specify a primary key, you give the keyword CONSTRAINT, followed by a name for the constraint. The constraint is named so that it can be referred to later and deleted and replaced if necessary. The name is followed by the keywords PRIMARY KEY. Finally, the column that will serve as the primary key is given inside parentheses.

The fourth line in the RoleQuote table definition in Example Query 6-5 shows how a concatenated primary key—a key based on more than one column—can be defined. This line is similar in form to the definition of a one-column primary key. The difference is that two primary key columns are included inside the parentheses, separated by commas:

```
CONSTRAINT RoleQuotePK PRIMARY KEY (roleID, quoteID)
```

The fifth line of the RoleQuote table definition in Example Query 6-5 is representative of how a foreign key can be defined:

```
CONSTRAINT RoleFK FOREIGN KEY (roleID) REFERENCES Role
  (roleID)
```

To specify a foreign key, you use the keyword CONSTRAINT, followed by a name for the constraint. The constraint is named so that it can be referred to later and deleted and replaced if necessary. It is followed by the keywords FOR-EIGN KEY. The column in the RoleQuote table that is the foreign key column, roleID, is given in parentheses; it is followed by the keyword REFERENCES. Next, the name of the corresponding primary key table, Role, is given. The primary key column of that table, which also happens to be named roleID, is given in parentheses. The RoleQuote table definition illustrates the fact that a column may be both a foreign key and part of the primary key at the same time.

Unfortunately, although the Microsoft Access documentation indicates that the FOREIGN KEY definition syntax works, depending on your installation and version, you may find that when you try to execute these statements you get an error message. If that is the case, then you must remove the foreign key constraints from the commands before running them successfully. If you were creating a database of your own that required foreign key constraints, you could still add them through the graphical user interface, even if it was not possible to do so using SQL.

6.4 The Keywords INSERT INTO, VALUES, UPDATE, SET, and DELETE FROM

Once a table has been created, you can insert data into it using SQL. Example Query 6-6 is a representative command that would enter suitable data into the Actor table. In this insertion query, the keywords INSERT INTO are followed by the name of the table, Actor. This name is followed by the keyword VALUES and a pair of parentheses. Inside the parentheses, the data values for a row in the table are given in the same order as the columns of the table. Text values are surrounded by single quotes, and date values are enclosed by a pair of # symbols. If there is no value for a column, the keyword NULL is used.

Example Query 6-6

```
INSERT INTO Actor VALUES('00001', 'Hanks', 'Tom', NULL, NULL,
'M', #7/9/1956#, NULL);
```

It is also possible to change the data in a row using an SQL query. Example Query 6-7 would change Tom Hanks' last name in the Actor table. In this update query, the keyword UPDATE is followed by the name of the table, and the keyword SET is followed by the name of the column to change and the new value. The rest of the query uses syntax that you have seen before. The WHERE keyword allows you to specify which row to change. This very powerful syntax makes it possible to change more than one row at a time. You need to be careful if you use it, however: Once the change has been made, it can't be undone.

Example Query 6-7

```
UPDATE Actor
SET lastName = 'Hunks'
WHERE lastName = 'Hanks';
```

It is also possible to delete a row from a table using an SQL query. Example Query 6-8 would delete the row for Tom Hanks from the Actor table. In this deletion query, the keywords DELETE and FROM are followed by the name of the table to change. The WHERE keyword allows you to specify which row to delete. This very powerful syntax makes it possible to delete more than one row at a time. You need to be careful if you use it, however: Once the deletion has been made, it can't be undone.

If you want to update or delete many records at a time, then SQL is much easier to use than a graphical user interface. Conversely, if you want to work with only one row at a time, it can be more convenient to use a GUI.

Example Query 6-8

```
DELETE FROM Actor
WHERE lastName = 'Hanks';
```

Annotated Bibliography of References for the Example Database

Movie Information

The preferred source of information for the Movie table was the following book:

1. Osborne, Robert. *75 Years of the Oscar: The Official History of the Academy Awards.* Abbeville Press, New York/London, 2003.

   Reference 1 provided information on a movie's title, year, production company, total Academy Award nominations, and number of Academy Awards won. All of the information in printed reference 1 plus information on more recent movies can be found at *http://www.oscars.org.*

Except for recent movies, the award information can be cross-checked in the following source:

2. Mowrey, Peter C. *Award Winning Films: A Viewer's Reference to 2700 Acclaimed Motion Pictures.* McFarland and Co., Jefferson, North Carolina/London, 1994.

The information in the Movie table on the prices of DVD's was made up, but based on figures available on online retailers' web sites on June 9, 2008.

More Information on Movies and Information on Roles and Who Played Them

If a movie was listed at *http://www.oscars.org,* that was the preferred source of information for the Role table. That information can be cross-checked in the printed references given below. If a movie was not listed at *http://www.oscars*.org, then the following printed references were the preferred source of information.

1. *The American Film Institute Catalog of Motion Pictures Produced in the United States. Feature Films, 1931–40, Film Entries, A–L (vol. 1), Film*

Entries, M–Z (vol. 2). Patricia King Hanson, Executive Editor; Alan Gevinson, Associate Editor. University of California Press, Berkeley/Los Angeles/Oxford, 1993.

2. *American Film Institute Catalog of Motion Pictures Produced in the United States. Feature Films, 1941–1950, Film Entries, A–L (vol. 1), Film Entries, M–Z (vol. 2).* Patricia King Hanson, Executive Editor; Amy Dunkleberger, Assistant Editor. University of California Press, Berkeley/Los Angeles/Oxford, 1999.

3. *The American Film Institute Catalog of Motion Pictures, Feature Films 1961–1970.* Richard P. Krasfur, Executive Editor. R. R. Bowker Company, New York/London, 1976.

4. *International Dictionary of Films and Filmmakers–1: Films, 2nd ed.* Nicholas Thomas, Editor; James Vinson, Consulting Editor. St. James Press, Chicago/London, 1990.

For movies not listed at *http://www.oscars.org* and more recent than the dates of these reference sources, information found at *http://www.imdb.com* was used.

Actor Information

The preferred source of information for the Actor table was the following book:

1. *Leonard Maltin's Movie Encyclopedia.* Leonard Maltin, Editor; Spencer Green and Luke Sader, Co-editors. Dutton, Penguin Group, New York, 1994.

If an actor didn't appear in reference 1, this source was used:

2. Katz, Ephraim; revised by Fred Klein and Ronald Dean Nolan. *The Film Encyclopedia, 4th ed.* HarperResources, New York, 2001.

If an actor didn't appear in reference 1 or 2, but a date of birth or death could be found at *http://www.imdb.com*, that date was used. If all that could be found was a year and not a complete date, then the date column for that actor was left blank in the database.

Information on Quotes and Who Spoke Them

The preferred source of information for the Quote and RoleQuote tables was the American Film Institute's list of the 400 quotes nominated for the "100 Years . . .100 Movie Quotes" list, available at *www.afi.com. Except for recent movies, this information can be cross-checked in this source:*

1. Nowlan, Robert A., and Gwendolyn W. Nolan. *Film Quotations: 11,000 Lines Spoken on Screen, Arranged by Subject, and Indexed.* McFarland and Co., Jefferson, North Carolina/London, 1994.

Some information was also verified by borrowing a copy of the movie and listening to the lines as spoken, checking the credits, and so on.